52
BOXES
IN 52 WEEKS

52 BOXES

IN 52 WEEKS

IMPROVE YOUR DESIGN SKILLS
ONE BOX AT A TIME

MATT KENNEY

The Taunton Press, Inc., 63 South Main Street, PO Box 5506, Newtown, CT 06470-5506
Email: tp@taunton.com

Editor: Peter Chapman
Copy Editor: Seth Reichgott
Jacket/Cover design: Guido Caroti
Interior design: Rita Sowins
Layout: Rita Sowins
Photographer: All photos by Matt Kenney, except: Kelly Dunton: pp. 17 (except photo 5), 22, 25–26, 28–33, 35, 74, 80, 109, 137, 148, 174, 180–81, 193, 206–207; Dillon Ryan: pp. 17 (photo 5), 18, 20–21
Illustration: Christopher Mills

The following names/manufacturers appearing in *52 Boxes in 52 Weeks* are trademarks: 3M®, Craigslist®, DeWalt®, eBay®, Forstner®, Lie-Nielsen®, Photoshop®, Sakura®, Waterlox®, Zinsser®

Library of Congress Cataloging-in-Publication Data

Names: Kenney, Matt, author.
Title: 52 boxes in 52 weeks : improve your design skills one box at a time / Matt Kenney.
Other titles: Fifty-two boxes in fifty-two weeks
Description: Newtown, CT : The Taunton Press, Inc., [2018] | Includes index.
Identifiers: LCCN 2017050134 | ISBN 9781631868924
Subjects: LCSH: Woodwork. | Wooden boxes. | Box making.
Classification: LCC TT197.5.B68 K46 2018 | DDC 745.51--dc23
LC record available at https://lccn.loc.gov/2017050134

Printed in the United States of America
10 9 8 7 6 5 4 3 2

DEDICATION

FOR GRACE AND ELIJAH. WORK HARD AND BELIEVE IN YOURSELF. YOU'LL GET WHERE YOU WANT TO GO.

ACKNOWLEDGMENTS

Had you asked me 20 years ago, when I was a graduate student studying philosophy, if I'd like to write a book, I would have said, "Definitely," and "About Plato's *Symposium*." Well, I've written a book, but it's about a bunch of boxes I made during the course of a year. For that, I owe thanks to many people. First, to my parents, Bill and Pat Kenney, who taught me that goals are achieved through dedication, work, believing in yourself, and being stubborn enough not to listen to anyone who tells you no. I am eternally grateful for the kindness, lumber, and shop time given to me by Joe Mazurek. He taught me to make furniture. The boxes in this book would not be what they are without Mike Pekovich, who patiently lent an ear whenever I wanted to talk design and technique. I'm also thankful for the rest of my work family at *Fine Woodworking*. I am fortunate to work with such smart, insightful, and kind folks. They never got tired of me bringing in yet another box. That they actually liked them was wonderful and encouraging as well. As for you, Anissa, thanks for keeping them so well organized and safe after I was done. Finally, thanks to everyone who read along as I made and then wrote about the boxes on my blog. I never expected much of anyone to take an interest, but I am pleased that so many did.

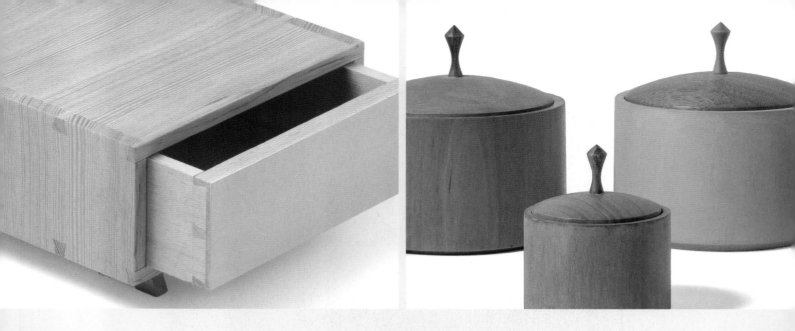

CONTENTS

INTRODUCTION

I played baseball when I was a kid. Here's what I learned from my dad about how to get better at hitting, base running, catching fly balls, and everything else baseball related: Practice. Do it over and over and over until it becomes second nature.

Woodworking is no different. If you want to cut better dovetails, then you've got to get into the shop and cut them. Then cut some more. After that, cut several hundred more. Repeat for several years or a decade. Now you're cutting dovetails like Christian Becksvoort.

I've always worked on my dovetails and all the other joinery used in furniture making. It helps, and I've gotten better. However, there is a skill that I did not practice enough: design. Good design, I believe, is an acquired skill. Sure, it helps if you've got some natural talent, but it's not necessary. You can still create beautiful furniture of your own design if you work at it hard enough and for long enough. (You should, of course, practice good design over and over. There are some principles and concepts that can help you in that regard. I'll come back to them throughout this book, to share my limited knowledge of them.) So, I set a challenge for myself: Design and make 52 boxes in 52 weeks.

What did I hope to accomplish throughout the year? Primarily, I wanted to jump-start the growth of my design aesthetic, helping it move more quickly toward maturity. Making 52 boxes in 52 weeks also would hone my woodworking chops. So, after a year of near nonstop building, did I meet my goals? I know I refined my technical skills. I was making tighter joints, and applying finishes better than I had before. I also think my design skills improved, and that my aesthetic grew by leaps and bounds.

I should point out that I didn't actually make a box every week. Because I often travel for work, occasionally get corralled into acting foolish in front of a video camera, and generally have a busy life, there was no way I could do that. Sometimes I knocked out a box in a few days. Sometimes it was several in a week. One box took me eight weeks to complete. As I set out on the challenge, I knew I wouldn't end up with 52 unique boxes. I made several iterations of certain designs, each time changing the wood used for the body or the paint for the lid (or making some other such change), to determine which I liked best. Or I occasionally modified a design until I came to a fully resolved version of it.

I originally documented the 52 boxes on a blog on my website: www.mekwoodworks.com. You can also find many more photos of my work on Instagram @kenney.matt.

Looking back, I am happy I did this, even though it was tough at times (like when it was below 40°F in my unheated New England shop). Sure, my personal growth as a maker and designer is satisfying, but perhaps even more satisfying is that many other woodworkers have told me that they benefited from the project as well. It opened their eyes to new possibilities in design and construction. That's wonderful. I am always eager to share my passion for this craft with others, and if it has sparked a passion in at least a few, then I've achieved something far better than what I had set out to accomplish.

ON DESIGN

A fair amount of time has passed since I completed Box 52, and I've thought quite a bit about what I was up to as I designed the boxes. I don't know if I learned a lot about design in some grand sense while I was making these 52 boxes, but I did figure out a ton about how I design. I gained clarity about what matters to me in design, and about the process by which I design. I also developed some details that are now characteristic of my work. That's what I was after when I started, so I think the project was a success.

Although I am not unique in this regard, my overall goal when designing is to create a harmonious, elegant box, one with quiet beauty. As I work toward this goal, six distinct but related things occupy my mind: overall proportion, simplicity, ensuring that the details of a box are proportionate to its overall size, developing details as fully as possible, choosing the best wood possible for a particular box, and utilizing color to emphasize the box's design. I'll do my best to explain these goals to you here.

Keep in mind that I'm describing how I design, not how all design happens, and certainly not how you ought to design. Still, these principles are not so tied to my design aesthetic that you couldn't employ them and produce boxes, or furniture, completely unlike mine. In fact, if you were to do this, I would be far more pleased than if you simply made a copy of one of my boxes.

Determine proportions first. Get them right and the box is off to an excellent start, but if they're wrong, the box is doomed.

GOOD PROPORTIONS ARE CRITICAL

When it comes to boxes (and furniture in general), nothing is more important than choosing a length, width, and height that work harmoniously together. A box should be so well proportioned that a person who comes across it, who stops to look at it and perhaps pick it up, should never even think about how the length, width, and height relate to one another. If you hit the proportions spot on, they step back, becoming a strong but quiet foundation for beauty.

So, how do you get there? A good place to start is with the old design chestnuts of the golden ratio and Fibonacci sequences, but they really are just a starting point. If you rely too heavily upon them, you can end up with boxes that are clunky. I learned this lesson many years ago when designing a box using the golden ratio to determine all of the dimensions. The width and length are great, but the box ended up being too tall. It looks like a little fat toad. I remade the box, making it wider and longer, with the width and length related by the golden ratio, but significantly shorter.

Now I use the golden ratio as a rough guide to determine two of the three dimensions. Which two? That depends on whether the box will be seen primarily from the top or the front. If from the top, I use the ratio for the width and length, but if from the front, it's the length and height. Still, the ratio is only a starting place. Tweak either dimension to get something a bit more pleasing to your eye, or perhaps more important, useful for the intended purpose of the box. As long as you are in the ballpark of the golden ratio, or rather on the infield in the ballpark, you'll be fine.

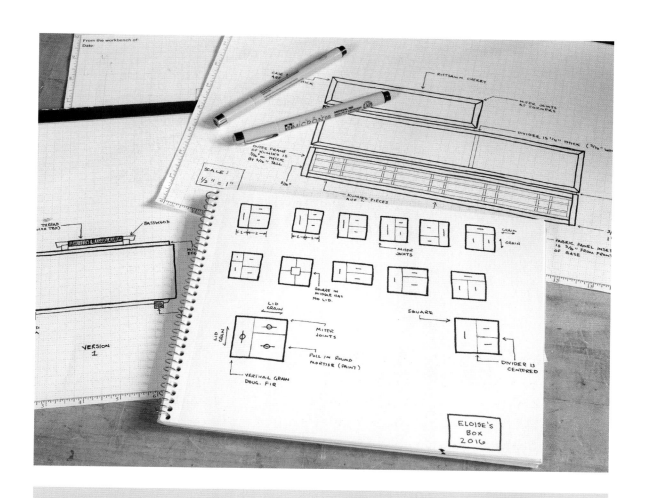

DESIGNING IN TWO DIMENSIONS

Here's an interesting note about how I design that's related to how I use the golden ratio. I always begin designing a box by considering only the face (top or front) that will be seen first. I work on the proportions, the arrangement of the compartments or drawers, the sizes of the various boxes when making a set of boxes grouped or stacked together, etc. I play with these elements to create a pleasing pattern and proportions. Only then do I move on to the third dimension.

Make it beautiful, not busy. Push your creativity by eliminating unnecessary ornamentation.
Get simple right and you'll have a beautiful box.

SIMPLE IS BEAUTIFUL

As I developed my sense of proportion, I discovered a wonderful thing: Beautiful boxes don't need adornment. I began to strip away everything that I could, leaving just the proportions, the clean lines, the geometry of the shapes, and the color of the wood. These elements can carry a box. Now I pursue simplicity with a passion. I'm obsessed with making something truly beautiful using as few elements as possible. This limited focus actually makes good design easier, because you don't wander aimlessly through option after option. Instead, you work within the constraints and begin to see new ways to employ them. You become more creative. You master a limited set of design details rather than moving from one to another without ever gaining an understanding of how they can be used to make a beautiful box. Pick one or two elements of a box to focus on, and work them over and over, asking yourself, "How can I use them differently?" This will force you to be creative, and you'll become a better designer as a result.

SMALL BOXES NEED SMALL PULLS

Many of my boxes are small, but not just in their overall dimensions. Everything about them is small. All the elements of a box—from its length, width, and height to the thickness of its sides and the size of its pull—should fit together harmoniously. Good proportions extend beyond basic dimensions. My smallest boxes have sides that are just ³⁄₁₆ in. thick, and as the size of the box grows, so too does the sides' thickness. I size pulls in proportion to the box's size as well. This need to make all parts of a box so that they strike a harmony when taken together is often overlooked. I've seen small boxes with thick sides and big, meaty pulls. It doesn't look right.

However, you should look beyond the size of the parts. The grain should be matched proportionally to the box. A short, little box needs really tight grain. If there are just a few, widely spaced grain lines running along the side, or, even worse, some nasty flatsawn cathedrals, the sides will look like a section of a big board. If the grain is tight and straight, then the side will look like it's just a normal board from a little tree. That might seem a bit absurd, but it really does make a difference.

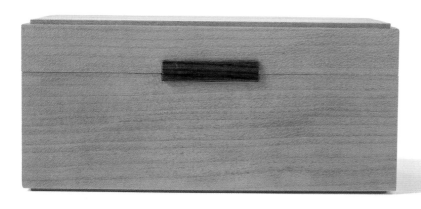

Work in scale. Every detail of a box, from grain to pull, should be sized to complement the box's proportions.

DEVELOP THE DETAILS

There's more to a box than its overall dimensions and the pull you pop on the lid, and you really can't stop designing until you have considered and worked out everything about it. When I make a box with a lid that fits into a rabbet cut into the top edge of the sides, I think carefully about how wide the rabbet should be, because this determines how thick the top edge of the side appears. I also consider how thick to make the top, because this determines how far the top rises above the sides. These are small things, but they definitely affect the box's appeal and beauty. The goal is for every detail of a box to be the result of forethought. Think carefully about the joinery. If you are going to use miters, you should have a good explanation for why. Are you going to angle the ends of the pull? Fine. Why? And are they going to angle down or up? Have an answer. This is how you arrive at a fully realized design, at a good design. It's a hard thing to do, because it requires discipline. Like you, I want to jump right into the making, but you have got to resist that urge until you know exactly where you are going and how you are going to get there. This knowledge comes from mapping out all the details beforehand.

BE THOUGHTFUL ABOUT WOOD

You know that bin of scrapwood over in the corner of your shop collecting dust? Do not look through it to find wood for your next box. Don't limit yourself to weird offcuts and odd-shaped chunks of funky exotic woods. The species of wood you use, its color, its cut of grain, the tightness of the grain, the size of the pores—these are all things you must consider when picking a board for the box. You must be just as fussy about the wood as you were about the design. It's all of a piece. I never go to the scrap bin. I do have a stack of small boards that I set aside because I know they have the qualities I look for when making a box, but again, I was deliberate about what I set aside. However, I am more likely to buy an 8/4 or 12/4 flatsawn board and rip it into thin boards as I need them, where the edge of the original board becomes the face of the new one. This creates a board that has tight riftsawn grain, and I can control every aspect of the wood I'm using.

Be picky. The wood you use to make a box is critical. Take your time and find the right piece, the one that enhances the box's design.

Think it through. Don't stop designing until you consider every aspect of a box, right down to grain orientation and the size of the pulls.

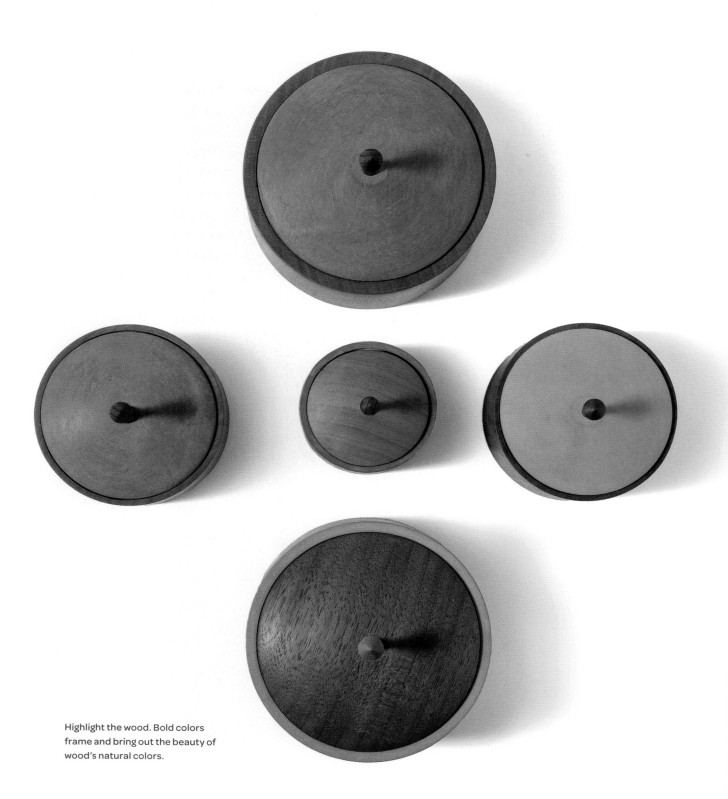

Highlight the wood. Bold colors
frame and bring out the beauty of
wood's natural colors.

EMBRACE COLOR

There's no way to slide quietly into this one. I use paint and fabric when I make boxes. They are as important to my design aesthetic as is my use of riftsawn domestic hardwoods (cherry, walnut, white oak, maple, etc.). More than a few grizzled woodworkers have turned their eyes from my boxes because of this. Happily, a great many more have told me that they love the bright colors I incorporate into my boxes. Why do I do it? To my eye the addition of color through paint and fabric gives the boxes an extra shimmer of life. It adds a touch of modernity to a traditional material and softens an otherwise muscular material just enough to give it a welcoming warmth.

I am particular about paint. I use only milk paint. Unlike latex paint (even matte latex paint), milk paint is not uniform in color. It has a wonderfully variegated color. There's almost a texture to it. This gives it the feel of a natural material. Wood, too, varies in color, even within the same board. Set against the earthy, warm, and organic surfaces of wood, latex paint is out of place. Milk paint is another story altogether. It's just as organic, so even though there might be a stark contrast between the bright color of the paint and the deep, rich color of wood, the two seem tied to one another.

A note about how I use milk paint: It's a traditional material that has been used in furniture making for centuries, but I've always used it in nontraditional ways. I paint a lid, or just the edges of a lid, maybe the feet of a pull. I like to paint the inside surface of a box's bottom, so that when you open the box there's an unexpected pop of color. It also brightens the box's interior. This gives my boxes a modern feel, even though I am using traditional materials to make them.

SOFTEN THE INSIDE

Now, about fabric. I first started to use fabric on the inside of boxes several years before I began the 52 boxes project. I like it for the same reason I like to paint the interior surface of a box bottom. It's a wonderful and unexpected splash of color. I also like that it takes the edge off the wood. Wood is a strong and dominant material. Combining it with fabric, often a small floral print, makes it less so.

However, I am rigorous in how I use fabric. First, it must be tight and fitted. There are no cushions beneath it. And the pattern on the fabric absolutely must fit proportionally with the size of the box. A small box demands a small print. If you open a small box and see just part of a very large floral print, something seems off. Open a small box and see a tiny floral print repeated many times within the box, and all seems right. The color of the fabric should complement the color of the wood, too. Stark contrast isn't good. As with all that I do, subtlety rules the day.

More inviting. Wood is wonderful, but it's hard and can be cold. A bit of fabric is a warm welcome and gives the box a gentle feel.

BOX-MAKING TECHNIQUES

I approach the process of making boxes the same way I approach designing them. Keep it simple, clean, and precise. An understated but elegant box should not be difficult to make, nor should it be made sloppily. That, as they say, is the sticky wicket. I've given a ton of thought to how I make boxes, and I've tried another ton's worth of techniques. I think I've finally gotten a handle on it. What I'll show you here isn't anything magical or especially difficult. In fact, it's all fundamental woodworking. The techniques I use to make boxes are elegant, and tremendously versatile. Use them and you're not confined to making boxes that look like mine. What I like most about the techniques I use is that they don't get in the way. They aren't flashy. When I look at a completed box, I don't get caught up by an insanely complex corner joint and a set of wickedly curvaceous legs. I see a beautiful box. That's what it's all about. Make something that evokes this reaction: Wow. That's beautiful. Anything else is unimportant.

THE BASICS OF BOX MAKING:
RESAWING, MITERS, AND STRONG JOINTS

There are many things that I obsess about when making a box, but none more so than grain that wraps seamlessly around all four corners of the box. It's a small detail, but one that can be the difference between a really good box and one that sings beautifully. It's less important on boxes that have dovetails, rabbets, and finger joints at the corners. It's absolutely necessary on a mitered box. When the grain swings uninterrupted around the joint, a lovely, harmonious cosmic music strikes up and warms your soul. If the grain comes to a stop on one side and is met by unmatched grain on the other side of the joint, small children cry for their mothers for fear that the end times are nigh. Perhaps I exaggerate, but continuous grain does look far better than grain that breaks at the corner.

1. Set the bandsaw fence to cut the board a little thicker than the side's final thickness.

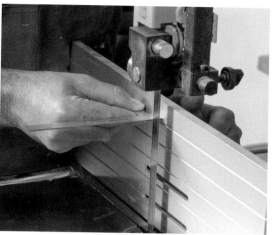

2. Check to make sure the fence face is parallel to the blade.

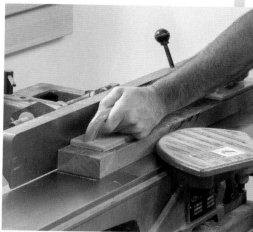

3. Joint one face of the board.

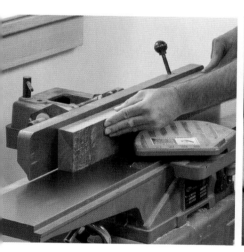

4. Joint one edge.

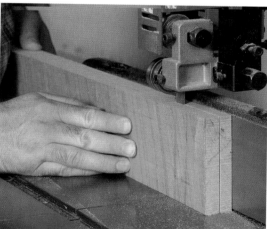

5. Resaw the first new board.

6. Re-joint the original face with a No. 5 jack plane.

Make two boards from one for perfect grain

The question, then, is how to create a box with grain that flows continuously around all four corners in an unbroken loop. The answer is resawing. Start with a thick board, at least 5/4 thick. Slice it down the middle at the bandsaw. The newly sawn faces of the two new boards become the outside of the box. What were the outside faces of the original board become the inside. Open the board like a book, but with the binding along the short edge. Hinge the boards at one end. See how the grain flows from one board to the next? That's the secret to a four-corner match. Make a

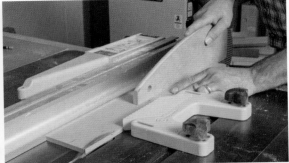

7. Adjust the sides up and down until the grain aligns along the two boards.

8. Trim excess width from the overhang of one board.

joint there and you have continuous grain. Another joint will come a bit farther in the board, and you'll get grain match there, too. The same goes for the second board. Now we have grain match at three corners. And just like the grain matched at the end where the two boards first met, it will match at the other end after you've cut out the sides (if you cut them out the correct way). That's the fourth corner. Now you've got grain running continuously around all four joints.

There's more to it than that, certainly, but it's all manageable. Here's how I do it. Starting with a thick board, I joint one face and one edge. I then set up my bandsaw to cut about ⅛ in. thicker than the final thickness of the box's sides and resaw a new board. I clean up the sawn face on the original board with a jack plane, taking very light shavings until all the sawmarks are just gone. This might seem a bit fussy, but the less material you remove from the bandsawn faces, the better that grain match will be at the corners. I then cut a second board. I joint the bandsawn face of the first new board cut, then take both of them to my planer and take them down to ⅟₃₂ in. over their final thickness. This extra bit of material lets me plane both surfaces to remove the machine marks.

At this point, the grain match at the corners where the two different boards meet will be close, but not perfect. Here's how I dial it in. Lay the boards down, outside faces up, so that they butt against one another end to end. Shift one board up and down until its grain lines up with the other. One board will end up lower than the other. Trim the bottom of that board so that the bottom edges on both pieces align. Next, rip both pieces to final width, placing the bottom edges against the rip fence. Once the pieces are mitered, the grain should wrap around the box perfectly.

A SLED FOR CROSSCUTS AND MITERS

Kenney uses a single sled for both square and mitered crosscuts. The key is a single rail that can be used in either miter-gauge slot. He has a right-tilt saw; those with left-tilt saws should reverse the sides of the sled.

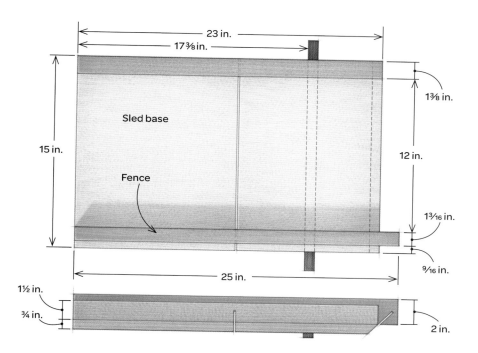

23 in.
17⅜ in.
Sled base
Fence
15 in.
12 in.
1⅜ in.
1³⁄₁₆ in.
⁹⁄₁₆ in.
25 in.
1½ in.
¾ in.
2 in.

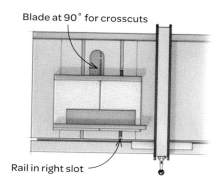

Blade at 90° for crosscuts

Rail in right slot

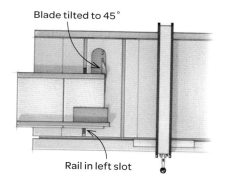

Blade tilted to 45°

Rail in left slot

CUTTING SEQUENCE

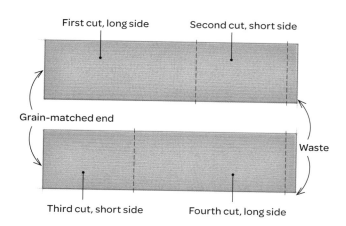

First cut, long side

Second cut, short side

Grain-matched end

Waste

Third cut, short side

Fourth cut, long side

Cut the sides to length, then miter them

Before I cut the sides to length, I cut the rabbet for the top and bottom. Then it's time for the miters. As simple a joint as a single miter is, it can be infuriating to get right. After cutting them by hand and machine a dozen different ways, I've settled on a method that gives perfect results, and I use it for all but the smallest boxes (I use hand tools for those). I cut them in two steps at the tablesaw with a sled that crosscuts and miters.

Begin by cutting the sides to length using a stop block to ensure that parallel parts are the same length. The two boards will each yield one long and one short side. It's important to cut each board starting from the same end to make sure the grain stays matched around the box.

What I'm about to explain might sound complicated, but check out the bottom drawing on p. 19; it shows what I'm doing. Set up a stop block for the long side and put the matched end of one board against the stop. Cut the first long piece and then set up another stop to cut the short side of that board (keep the first stop in place). Use the same stop to cut the short side of the next board, placing the matched grain end against the stop. Finally, remove the stop for the short sides and cut the last long piece.

To cut the miters, tilt the blade to 45°, put the sled in the opposite miter slot, and cut a kerf in the sled fence. Set a short side on the sled and move it up until the top corner of the end is right next to the kerf. Clamp a stop block against the other end. When you make the cut, the blade will cut the miter, but won't shorten the side, which will preserve the grain match. After making the first cut, turn the side end for end and cut the second miter. Repeat for the second short side and then miter the long sides in the same way, moving the stop block as needed.

The box sides are now mitered at 45° and the components are all set for glue-up. Any inside surface should be sanded or planed and finished before moving on.

1. With a stop block clamped to the crosscut sled, cut the box sides to length.

2. With the top corner of the side aligned with the edge of the kerf in the sled fence, cut the miters at the tablesaw.

1. Mix the glue size using equal parts yellow glue and water.

2. Spread the size on the mitered joints.

3. Keeping the two mitered tips tight together, tape up the first joint.

4. Carefully spread glue over the miter joints, except the open ends.

5. Place the top and bottom in the grooves in the sides and fold the sides around them. Before closing the final corner, apply glue to the miter faces there.

6. Stretch tape over the last mitered corner to apply clamping pressure.

Glue size makes for stronger joints

Gluing up end-grain miters on a box like this can pose some interesting issues, such as how to keep the end grain from soaking up the glue and starving the joint, or how to accurately keep pressure on all four miters while keeping the joints square.

To help avoid glue starvation, coat all of the joints with glue size using a small brush and let it dry before assembly. Glue size is a mixture of equal parts yellow glue and water that saturates and clogs the end grain. Let it dry for two hours before gluing up the box. Now, a full-strength glue spread won't wick into the end-grain fibers, and the resulting joint will be solid.

The best way to clamp a mitered box while keeping it square is with painter's tape. Lay out all four sides, miters face-up and touching, with the top and the bottom pieces within reach. Put tape on one side of the joint with enough overhang for the mating piece. With the mating piece vertical, press the mitered points together, then lay the piece flat. Now when the joint closes, the tape will stretch, keeping the joint tight and in line while the glue dries.

1. Mark the depth of the rabbet on the auxiliary fence.

2. Clamp the auxiliary fence to the tablesaw's rip fence.

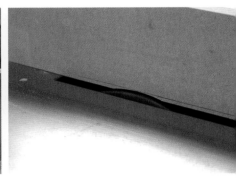

3. Raise the dado head until it reaches the mark on the auxiliary fence.

4. Set the fence to cut the width of the rabbet.

5. Cut the rabbet.

6. Use a shooting board to fit the lid.

LIDS THAT DON'T NEED HINGES

There was no way that I was going to make 52 boxes with hinged lids. I always use good hardware, and a good pair of box hinges costs around $30. I couldn't afford to put hinges on too many boxes. I also just don't like box hinges. I find them clunky. So, I decided not to use any hinges. (Box 45 on p. 169 has a hinged door, but that doesn't count.) Still, the lid needs to stay on the box. For the most part, I used one of three techniques to secure the lid. I dropped it into a rabbet, turned the lid into a box that fit over the bottom, or used a liner inside the bottom to grab the top. A few times I did away with the lid altogether and used a drawer or two instead.

Drop the top into a rabbet

I love this method of making a lid without hinges. It's wonderfully simple, but can be used to create elegant lines and depth, resulting in a more appealing box. I used it on 21 of the 52 boxes.

SHOOTING BOARD

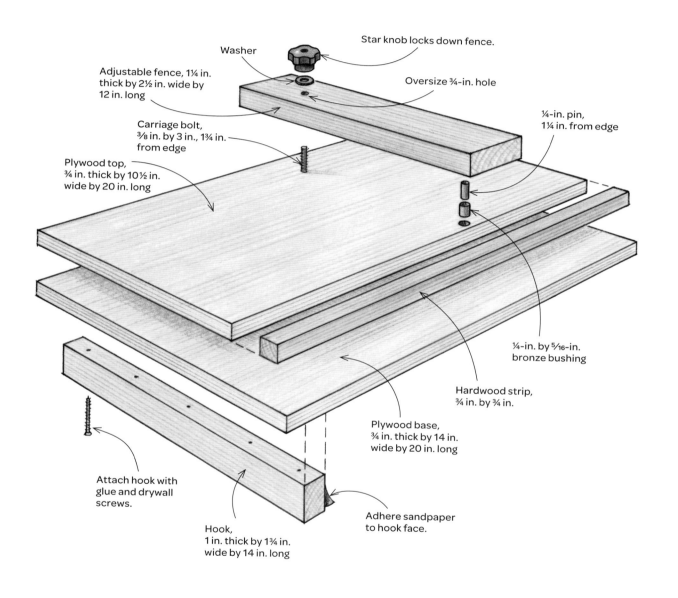

Washer

Star knob locks down fence.

Adjustable fence, 1¼ in. thick by 2½ in. wide by 12 in. long

Oversize ¾-in. hole

Carriage bolt, ⅜ in. by 3 in., 1¾ in. from edge

¼-in. pin, 1¼ in. from edge

Plywood top, ¾ in. thick by 10½ in. wide by 20 in. long

¼-in. by 5⁄16-in. bronze bushing

Hardwood strip, ¾ in. by ¾ in.

Plywood base, ¾ in. thick by 14 in. wide by 20 in. long

Attach hook with glue and drywall screws.

Adhere sandpaper to hook face.

Hook, 1 in. thick by 1¾ in. wide by 14 in. long

The key to an attractive lid made this way is to cut a rabbet that's shallower than the lid is thick, so the lid sticks up above the top edge of the box. For very small boxes, like Box 1 on p. 38, I cut the rabbet 3/16 in. deep and made the top 1/4 in. to 5/16 in. thick, because I prefer the lid to stick up more than 1/16 in., but less than 1/8 in. As for the rabbet's width, it can be as narrow as 1/16 in. (in sides that are just 3/16 in. thick) or up to half the side's thickness.

Because this is such an uncomplicated lid style, it's also quite easy to make. Before I cut the sides to length, I cut the rabbet for the top (and the bottom, too) with a dado set at the tablesaw. In the past, I would use a rabbeting bit in my router table. I stopped, because it often chipped out the rabbet's corners when cutting against the grain. Ugly. The dado set never does that. After the rabbet has been cut and the box is glued together, I fit the lid. I use both solid wood and plywood for lids. Solid-wood lids need more room for expansion and contraction, so keep that in mind when fitting them. To fit the lids, I first cut them just a hair or two oversize in length and width at the tablesaw. Then, I trim them to fit one shaving at a time with my shooting board and a handplane. This is a nice way to do it, because if the box is a bit out of square, you can put a shim between the lid and the shooting board's fence to create sides that run parallel to the box's sides (a lid that's out of square just as the box is). You end up with even gaps around all four sides of the lid. It looks good, and no one will notice that the box is slightly out of square. Eventually you'll forget that it is, too.

Put a box inside a box

I first learned this technique for making a box from my friend and colleague at *Fine Woodworking*, Mike Pekovich. It's brilliant for its simplicity. It's one box made from two boxes. The top box is open on the bottom. The bottom box is open on the top and fits into the top box. Wait, that sounds complicated. It's not. Really. Here's how to make it.

I used this technique when making Box 25 on p. 89, and I started with the lid. The four sides are mitered together, and the top panel fits into a rabbet. After the lid is made, the bottom is made to fit it. Do this by fitting each side of the bottom into the lid one at a time, with square ends. They should just slide in, but not loosely. The action should be smooth. Next, miter the ends and glue the sides together. Let the glue dry overnight and pull off the tape. Try to fit the bottom into the lid. It won't fit. Never does. So, break out a handplane and plane the sides, removing equal amounts from opposite sides, until the bottom fits into the lid. When the fit gets close, I set the bottom on my bench and put the lid on top of it. What I want is the lid to float slowly down, cushioned by air. When you've got that, you're done. One note: If you are going to paint the bottom, as I did on Box 25, the fit should be one shaving past perfect at this point. The paint does add some thickness and will bring the fit back to just right.

1. Measuring from inside corner to inside corner, mark the length of the side of the box.

2. Trim the sides of the bottom box pieces to fit into the lid box.

3. Miter the sides.

4. Test the fit by placing the bottom box sides into the lid.

5. Plane the sides to fit into the lid box.

6. Slide the bottom box into the lid box.

Use a liner inside

This technique is probably as old as the hills, and I suspect that it's still in use because it works really well. I like it for that reason, but also because it's quick and easy to do, and looks pretty darn snazzy to boot. It's the perfect choice when you want the grain on the sides to flow onto the lid, because the lid is cut free from the sides after the box has been glued together. The liner is then fit into the box bottom and sticks up a bit past the top edge of the sides. The lid fits snugly over that lip and sits securely in place.

The work for this type of lid doesn't begin until after you've glued the box together. I also glue the bottom and top into their rabbets as well. You should have a sealed-up box. The first thing to do is cut the lid free from the box. Until a few years ago, I had seen this done only at the tablesaw. That's how I did it, too. It works, but no matter how well set up your saw is, and no matter how perfectly made the box is, there always seems to be small steps at the corners, because the table-saw blade did not cut in the same plane as you went around the box. Now I do it at my bandsaw,

1. Cut the lid off the box at the bandsaw.

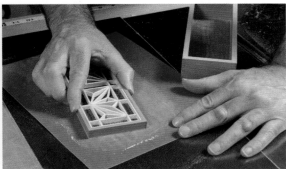

2. Sand the cut edges with a circular motion.

3. Using a miter shooting board, miter the sides of the liner.

4. Fit the liners into the box.

because I watched Mike Pekovich do this, and the lid and box go back together perfectly. It's the best way to do it, assuming you have a sharp blade on your saw and it's set up well. A bandsaw does leave a rough surface behind, so after you've cut the lid free, put a sheet of sandpaper on your tablesaw and sand the edges with a circular motion. I often start at 220-grit and move up to 400-grit. If the machine marks are particularly stubborn at 220-grit, I drop down to 180-grit, get rid of them, and then move back up.

Here's some advice about how to sand the edges and not muck them up. Sandpaper is a cutting tool, and like every other cutting tool, you'll get the best results when you let the tool do the cutting. Don't mash down on the box. Hold it gently, and sand it in about as big a circle as you can. Also, like every other cutting tool, if sandpaper is dull or its "teeth" are clogged with dust, it won't cut efficiently. Get out a new sheet.

After the edges are nice and clean, it's time to fit the liner sides. I'll tell you this: You should have a miter shooting board to do this. It's the best way to get the liners to fit with just the right amount of friction and tight joints. Start with a long side, fitting it with square ends and then mitering it. It should slide in with a hint of resistance but should not bow out in the middle. Do the other long side next. Now fit one of the ends. It should be tight but not so tight that it's hard to push in. Finally, fit the second end. Be careful here. I can't tell you how many times I've gotten the fit just a hair too tight and was unable to get the liners back out without extreme difficulty. As a precaution against this, I now plane both faces of the liners, and make sure the top edges are planed, too, before I fit the liners. This way, if they do get stuck, they are finished.

FORGET THE LID: USE A DRAWER INSTEAD

The third and fourth boxes I made didn't even have lids. They had drawers. I ended up making six boxes with drawers instead of lids, and they're all among my favorites. I have a soft spot for drawers because of how they can be used to create interesting patterns on the front of a box or piece of furniture. Also, I like that drawers are somewhat unexpected in boxes. The majority of boxes that I see—and that I make—have a lid, and the contrarian in me, which is rather large and very active, just wants to do something different. Drawers instead of a lid is different, so I like it. Perhaps what I'm getting at is don't let traditional box designs restrict what you make. Take a look at what's out there, and then do all that you can to run in another direction.

A STABLE AND VERSATILE BOTTOM

I used a variety of lid styles over the course of making these 52 boxes, but when it came time to make a bottom, I relied on one style over and over. At its heart is a thin sheet of plywood, either 3/16 in. or ¼ in. thick. Why plywood? Because it moves very little and can be glued into a rabbet without creating problems with wood movement. It's an easy bottom to make, but that's not the only reason I used it repeatedly. Most of my boxes are small and delicate, but because the bottom is glued to all four sides, they are rigid and strong. What's more, I like the aesthetic options a plywood bottom affords me. I can glue veneer to it, and fabric, too. I also can bring the edge of the bottom very close to the outside of the box, and paint it. Rather than an afterthought hidden beneath the box, the bottom becomes a means of strengthening a box's design. Solid-wood bottoms are less versatile, less stable, and don't add strength to the box because they must float free in a groove.

That's enough of the why. Let's get to the how. It all starts with a piece of plywood. I always glue a piece of veneer to what will be the bottom's outside face. Sometimes it's veneer that I bought

1. Resaw a veneer that's a little wider and longer than the plywood bottom.

2. Glue the veneer (smooth face down) to the outside face of the bottom.

3. Clamp between cauls, and allow an hour or two for the glue to dry.

4. Trim the veneer flush to the plywood.

(which is very thin), but more often than not it's veneer that I've sawn in my shop at the bandsaw. I prefer shopsawn veneer because I can cut it from the same board used to make the box. The grain and color match between the bottom and sides are then perfect. But I'm getting a bit ahead of myself. Back to the plywood. Cut it oversize. Next, cut a piece of veneer that's a bit wider and longer than the plywood. How thick? Well, the veneer should be no more than ⅛ in. thick, but you need some meat to work with, so it's OK to cut it ³⁄₁₆ in. thick for now.

When you make shopsawn veneer, you end with a thin piece of veneer that is smooth on one face (because it's been jointed so that you can run it against the saw's fence) and rough on the other from the bandsaw blade. Glue the smooth face to the plywood, with a bit of overhang on all four sides. Don't worry about the rough side, as it's easier to plane it smooth after it's been glued to the plywood. Give the glue an hour or two to dry, and then plane the veneer down to the plywood edges. After that, plane the rough side smooth, but just smooth enough to stick some tape to it (more on that later).

5. Fit the veneered bottom in the box.

6. Completely cover the veneer face with blue painter's tape.

7. Trim the tape flush with the edges of the bottom.

8. Paint the edges of the bottom with milk paint.

9. Remove the tape and plane the veneer after the milk paint dries.

Now is when you cut the bottom to size and fit it to the box. It's smart to wait to do this because you end up with cleaner edges. The next thing I do is paint the edges of the bottom with milk paint. I do it for two reasons. First, the paint covers up the plywood edge, but second, and more important, the milk paint is a nice detail. I begin by covering the entire surface of the veneer with blue tape. Cut the tape flush with the bottom's edges. Mix up the milk paint and paint the edges (I explain how to do this on p. 34). After you're done painting the edges, pull up the tape and plane the veneer again to clean up the surface. No matter how well you tape the veneer, there will be paint around the edges. Trust me. I know from experience. Bring the veneer down to at least ⅛ in., but preferably less.

The bottom is almost done, but the inside surface needs some attention. My favorite thing to do is to glue a piece of fabric to it, but you could paint it, too. (If you choose to paint the bottom, do so when you are painting the edges.) I love using fabric in my boxes, and I could spend hours in a quilt shop looking for new ideas. Wash your fabric and then iron it. Flip it over. Put the bottom, inside surface down, on the fabric. Trace around it with a thin-tip marker (I use a Sakura® Pigma

10. Trace around the bottom onto the fabric with a thin-tip marker.

11. Cut the fabric just inside the pen line.

12. Spray glue onto bottom.

13. Carefully lay down the fabric.

14. Apply a bead of glue to the rabbet in the box sides.

15. Press the bottom into the rabbet.

16. Using cauls to protect the edges, clamp the bottom to the box.

Micron 08 black pen). Using a pair of sharp scissors, cut out the fabric just inside the pen line. Spread some newspaper out on your bench and put the bottom on it, inside face up. Coat it with some spray adhesive, like 3M® 77 (available at home centers and hardware stores). Move the bottom away from the overspray and then lay the fabric down. I start at one end, holding the other end up with my right hand and using my left index finger to press the fabric down, running along the bottom's length. Be careful not to stretch it out. If you do, the fabric will overhang at the other end. Trim it back to the edge with your scissors.

Now pop the bottom in and turn the box over. Marvel at how clean it is. The line between the box sides and the fabric should be tight and beautiful—and much better than you get using a foam cushion covered in fabric. Glue in the bottom, using cauls to protect the bottom and top edge of the box. After the glue has dried, move on to the finish.

KEEP THE FINISH SIMPLE AND FAST

I think I've established by now that I like to keep things simple. This holds true when it comes to finishes for my boxes. Boxes are small, delicate things that sit and look pretty. Perhaps you open it once or twice a day to put a ring inside. Most likely you open it much less often. Boxes don't get handled much, so the finish doesn't need to be crazy thick and bombproof. Save the bowling alley finish and bar-top epoxy for another day—a day far, far off in the future, so that when you open the can it will be rock hard and unusable. Instead, get some shellac flakes and denatured alcohol. While you're at it, get some milk paint, too. As far as I'm concerned, these are the only two finishes you need for boxes. Shellac is easy to apply, and it's actually quite durable. Milk paint adds a pop of color that I just can't resist. There's one more thing you need for the finish: a good paste wax, one meant for furniture and not for bowling alleys and butcher blocks. (I'm sure those are great waxes, but just not for furniture.)

1. Plane the surface to get rid of machine marks.

2. Sand the surfaces, starting with 320-grit paper and working up as far as 600-grit (for highly figured woods).

The secret to a beautiful finish

Here's something that I learned a long time ago: The secret to success in any endeavor is always quite mundane and boring. I've run a lot in my life. You know the secret to running long distances quickly? It's running a lot. I mean a lot, like 70 or more miles a week. The secret is hard work. There are no shortcuts.

It's the same with beautiful finishes for boxes and furniture. The secret to a great finish is great surface prep. It's got to be flawless. And there are no shortcuts here, either. First, I sharpen either my smoothing plane or my low-angle block plane (the blade has a high angle so that the cutting angle is around 45 degrees, which is perfect for smoothing). Then, I plane the surface. This gets rid of machine marks and the like. If there is any tearout, then your plane isn't really sharp. This is true unless you're using some insanely figured wood, in which case you might need a higher effective cutting angle. With a bevel-up plane like a block plane, you can just hone the blade with a higher angle and try again.

After I've planed the surfaces, I break out the sandpaper. I start with 320-grit paper, which is effective at removing any tracks left by the plane. I then move on to 400-grit and, with especially figured woods, I'll go even farther up the grit ladder and pull out the 600-grit. Keep in mind that the secret to successful sanding is a light touch. After the sanding is done, it's time to apply a finish.

Shellac is simple, fast, and beautiful

When I first started to use shellac, I used a heavy cut of premixed shellac from a can. It was hard to apply cleanly, and I gave up on shellac. It wasn't until I learned to use a very light cut of shellac, taught to me by Mike Pekovich, that I finally understood the appeal of shellac. I prefer to use shellac flakes now and make my own, but for a long time I would buy a quart of Zinsser® SealCoat and mix it 50/50 with denatured alcohol to make a really light cut of shellac. So, you can do that if you don't want to do what I'm about to explain.

I make a ½-lb. cut of shellac. It's 1 oz. (by weight) of shellac flakes mixed with 4 oz. of denatured alcohol. I use super blonde dewaxed shellac flakes, because it's very clear and doesn't affect the wood's natural color much. Use a glass jar and pour the alcohol over the flakes. It takes a while for the flakes to dissolve, several hours at least. Make sure to shake the jar every now and then, but don't fret about how long it takes them to dissolve. In the meantime, you can prepare the box for the shellac (see the facing page), and then read a few issues of *Fine Woodworking* magazine.

1. Mix shellac flakes and alcohol.

2. Wipe on the first coat.

3. Apply a second coat and let dry.

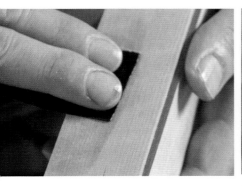

4. Wet sand with 800-grit wet/dry paper and mineral spirits. Apply a third coat and let dry.

5. Rub with extra-fine steel wool.

6. Finish by waxing all the shellacked surfaces.

Well, it's been a few hours. The shellac is completely dissolved, so it's time to get busy. Grab a bit of old T-shirt or some other soft fabric (preferably white and free of dyes), fold it up, and dip it into the shellac. Wipe it across the surface. Move around the box and get the edges, too, but don't do the bottom yet. Set the box down on the bottom and wait. You won't be waiting long. Shellac cut this light dries insanely fast. Give it five minutes. Now shellac the bottom and let it dry. Apply a second coat to all the surfaces and let it dry. Sand everything with 800-grit wet/dry sandpaper. I use mineral spirits to lubricate the paper and prevent the paper from clogging. Set the box aside and let the mineral spirits dry. Apply a third coat and let it dry. Take some extra-fine steel wool and rub it over all of the surfaces, which will knock the sheen off the shellac. Grab another piece of T-shirt and rub some wax over all the shellacked surfaces. I use Renaissance wax, because I love the soft luster it gives the wood. That's it. You're done.

Milk paint rocks

Ah. Milk paint. My beloved milk paint. I love the matte, mottled colors. I love that I can mix different colors to create new ones. I love that my use of paint upsets some folks who think you should never paint wood. As my wonderful grandfather Kenney would say, "Peshaw." I love the bold pop of color that milk paint gives. I love that it's a traditional finish from ye olde days of Colonial America but that I can use it in very untraditional ways. It's a glorious thing.

I've already explained how to apply milk paint to the edge of a bottom, but I didn't go into too much detail. Here's the technique I use for edges and larger surfaces.

Mix the paint first. I've found that warm water dissolves the powder better than cool or cold water. As for the ratio of water to powder, it's about 1 part powder to 1 part water. However, this is just a starting point. It varies from color to color, and even between bags of the same color. After mixing the powder and water, let the mixture sit for at least 20 minutes. At this point, I'm looking for the paint to be a bit thinner than latex paint. Once it's ready, applying milk paint is a lot like applying shellac. I apply a coat, let it dry, and then apply a second coat. After the second coat is dry, I sand with 320-grit paper. I then clean off the dust and apply a third coat. After the third coat is dry, I sand with 400-grit paper and clean off the dust. I then apply wax and I'm done.

1. Pour warm water into the powdered milk paint (about 1 part to 1 part).

2. Mix and then let the mixture sit for at least 20 minutes.

3. Apply the first coat and let dry.

4. Apply a second coat, let dry, and then sand with 320-grit paper.

5. Apply a third coat and let dry.

6. Sand with 400-grit paper.

7. Apply wax to finish.

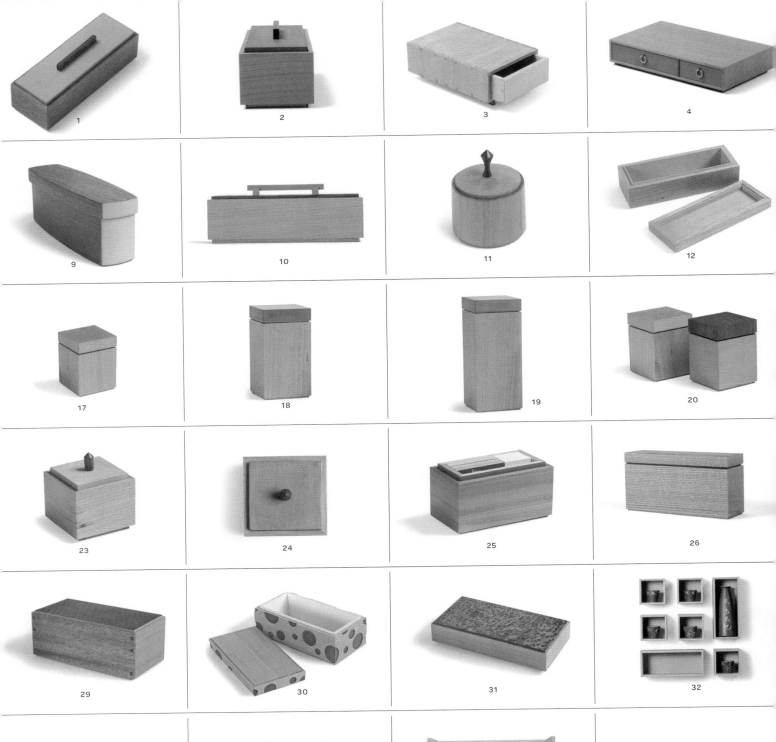

1

2

3

4

9

10

11

12

17

18

19

20

23

24

25

26

29

30

31

32

37

38

39

40

45

46

47

48

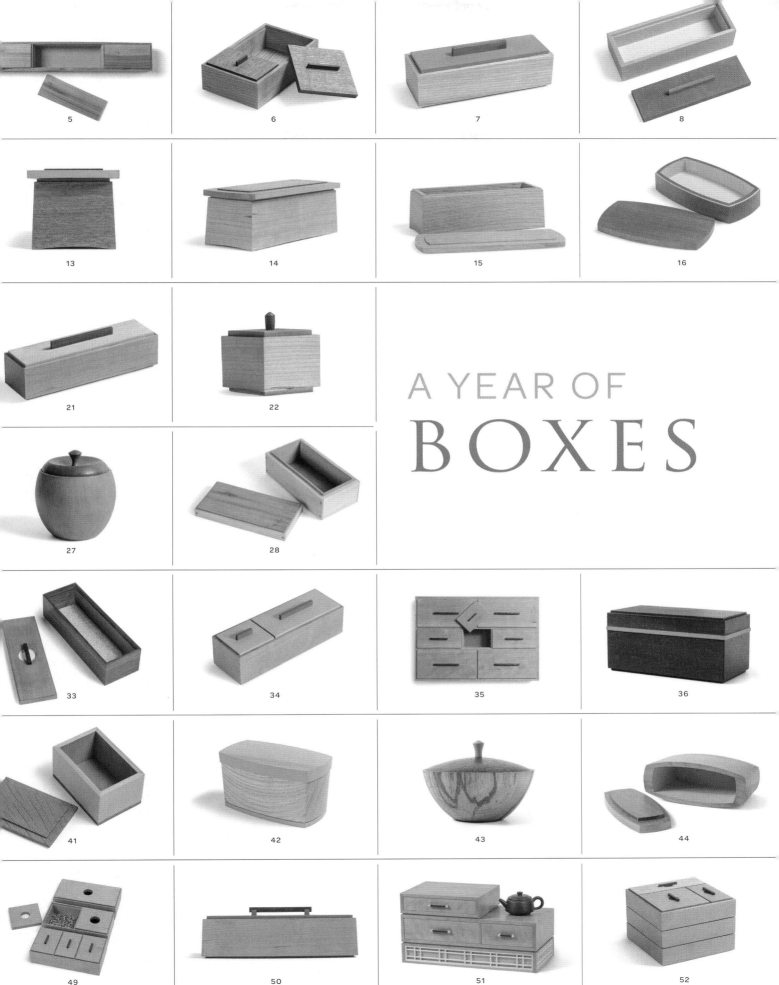

A YEAR OF
BOXES

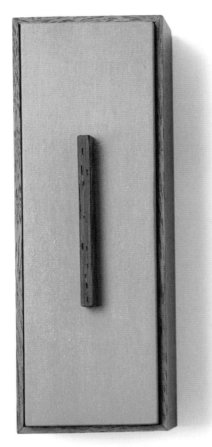

BOX 1

BOX 2

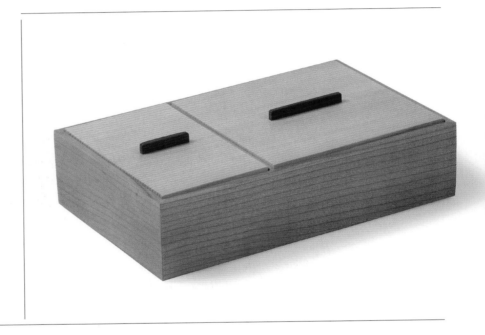

BOX 2

BOXES 1&2

To start things off, I wanted to make a small, delicate box. But then I thought the box would look nice as a pair, so I made one in walnut and one in cherry. I'm happy with how they turned out. Together, they make a bold graphic statement, and I think they should remain a pair.

The overall design is similar to other boxes that I've made, like the box with two compartments at center right on the facing page. The big difference is that this new box has a single, painted lid instead of two wooden lids finished with shellac.

I like the proportions: just over 1 in. tall, 1¾ in. wide, and 5 in. long. That's really small, but I think that I can go smaller. I should note that because the ends are so short, I cut the sides apart with a dozuki saw and squared up the ends at my shooting board. I then cut the miters with a shooting board, too. This technique resulted in a very good four-corner grain match, because cutting out the sides and mitering the ends removed very little material. (It also helps to start out by resawing with a thin-kerf bandsaw blade.)

SPECS		BOX 1	BOX 2
		› Walnut	› Cherry
		› Marigold yellow milk paint	› Federal blue milk paint
		› Wenge pull	› Cocobolo pull
		› 1½ x 1¾ x 5	› 1½ x 1¾ x 5

I also tried out a new technique on this box. On previous boxes I've made I used a solid-wood bottom that I rabbeted. The resulting tongue on the bottom's edge fits into a groove in the box sides. The sides of this little walnut box are far too thin (less than $\frac{3}{16}$ in.) to hold a groove. Instead, I rabbeted the bottom edge of the sides and glued the bottom into the rabbet. Don't worry, it's not a solid-wood bottom. I veneered a thin ($\frac{3}{32}$ in. thick) piece of walnut to each face of the plywood, trimmed them flush to the edges, and then glued walnut edging to all four sides. The walnut veneers were glued down perpendicular to the grain on the plywood's surface veneers. There won't be any seasonal wood movement, so there shouldn't be any problems. On the cherry box, I used cherry veneer and banding.

ATTACHING THE PULL

You could glue the pull to the lid, but there's always the risk that it might eventually come undone from the milk-painted lid. For added security, I drilled two pilot holes in the top, drove in some little brad nails, and snipped off their heads, leaving about ¼ in. of nail sticking out. I drilled holes in the pull, dropped some glue into the holes, and put the pull on the nails. It worked brilliantly.

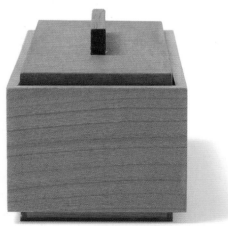

BOX 3

This box is a bit funky because the drawer opens from both ends. It's made from a wonderful, 10-in.-wide piece of vertical-grain Douglas fir. Given how tight the grain is, I'm guessing that it's old growth. I found the piece in a small lumberyard near my house. (Boards like it are why I drop into lumberyards on a whim and look around for hours.) Vertical-grain Douglas fir is one of my favorite woods.

I love the concept for this box: a drawer that slides out at both ends. I also like the feet, and that the box has a modern feel to it. These are strong enough to overcome some details that I'm not so happy with: The snow white milk paint turned out to have much less variation in color than other colors of milk paint that I've worked with, so it doesn't read as painted wood. Also, I didn't quite get the box's proportions right. On reflection, it should be shorter and wider. Finally, I should have gone with miters instead of dovetails. The box is too small for dovetails. They just crowd up the place and interrupt the flow of the fir's grain. But that's the way it goes sometimes. And we're only on Box 3.

| SPECS | > Vertical-grain Douglas fir
> Snow white milk paint
> 3¼ x 9 x 6

But let's get back to those feet. The gentle arc along the bottom is lovely, and the ends angle downward at the same angle as the dovetails (see the bottom photo on the facing page). That angle is repeated on the two cleats that hold the feet to the box, but inverted so that it goes up and out. Designing these feet was the easy part. It was much harder to figure out how I could attach them without creating a seasonal movement problem. The solution: Glue the cleats to the box aligned with the grain. They are notched to fit over the feet. The feet are nailed into one of the cleats but float free in the notches of the other cleat. This way, the box can expand and contract freely. Had the feet been nailed into the second cleat too, the fact that the feet aren't moving seasonally along their length would have eventually torn the box apart as it moved across its width.

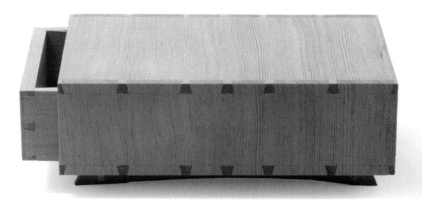

BOX 3 | 43

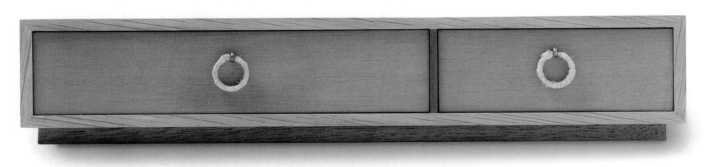

BOX 4

What a difference a week makes. Unlike Box 3, which I still have a hard time warming to, I like everything about this box. I know this one is quite different from last week's box, but I see the two as directly related. When thinking about how I'd change Box 3, I came up with Box 4. This is especially true in terms of the overall dimensions. Box 4 is about 3 in. narrower but twice as long (if you are reading width across the grain and length with the grain, which is how I do it). It's also much shorter. These are the proportions I had in mind when I first came up with the concept for Box 3. I don't know where or why I changed them on that box.

I also like a particular design leap that I made with Box 4: the walnut divider. Without even thinking about it, I have always made drawer dividers from the same species as the case or box. Most of the time, I think that's the right way to do it. But there is something very pleasing about this walnut divider paired with the white oak box. Perhaps it's the walnut base the box sits on, or that the divider is a preview of the beautiful walnut drawers inside. (By the way, this is all air-dried and unsteamed walnut. Hence the rich and variegated color. Steaming walnut destroys what's most beautiful about the wood. I'll never use it again, if I can avoid it.)

SPECS	> Quartersawn white oak	> Hemp twine
	> Walnut	> $2\frac{3}{8} \times 6\frac{7}{8} \times 12$
	> Custom green milk paint	

The pulls are made from key rings wrapped with a very thin hemp twine. I like them very much, even if there's a bit of a hump where I tied off the twine. I used cotter pins to attach them to the drawer fronts and blackened the pins with some chemical from a bottle; it's something used to darken the lead in stained glass. (I think it was also used by Sauron when he was crafting the one ring to rule them all. I'm sure it's not all that bad, but I have been referring to the box as my precious. And all of my other boxes are slowly beginning to turn invisible.)

The drawer boxes are walnut, mitered at the corners. I know this is a risk, but the drawers aren't going to be loaded down with gold bullion or lead. The painted fronts are white oak, which I chose because I knew the milk paint wouldn't completely cover the open grain of the oak. So you still get a hint of the oak through the paint. It looks nice. Also, the drawers are inset about $\frac{1}{16}$ in., to create some depth and to disguise the box's seasonal movement.

Finally, the base is a mitered frame screwed to the box. To accommodate seasonal movement, the pieces on the sides are cut a bit short (you can't see this unless you really look, because the darkness of the gap blends well with the darkness of the walnut).

BOX 5

The idea for this box has been floating around in my head for quite some time. I had not made it yet because every time it surfaced I couldn't get the proportions right. But inspiration often comes when we are least looking for it. After I had completed Box 4, I put it on the counter, knelt down in front of it to get a head-on look at the front elevation, and it hit me. Those were the perfect dimensions for this box. The length and width of this box are the same as the length and height of Box 4.

When I thought of this box in the past, I never had particular species in mind for the sides and lids. As I was looking through my lumber rack and assorted piles of small pieces of lumber, I took a break to go into the house and see what the kids were doing. My daughter was in her room, which is where I saw a little wall cabinet I made several years ago. It's ash and apple. The apple is gorgeous. I immediately decided to make the lids from apple. And the piece I found for this box is awesome. Look at those colors. Happily, I was able to mill the piece so that each lid contains a small "defect" in roughly the same area (see the top photo on p. 48). When viewed from the top, the lids look like little framed paintings. The box is subdued enough to let the lids stand out in all their beauty. (Apple could be the prettiest wood there is. Madrone is a close second. Sadly, my stash of apple got a bit smaller with this box.)

| SPECS | > Quartersawn white oak | > Marigold yellow milk paint |
| | > Apple | > 2 x 2 x 12 |

"Inspiration often comes when we are least looking for it."

I thought about making the body from ash, but back in my shop I came across a very nice piece of quartersawn white oak that was just the right size for the sides. The earthy, multi-hued apple, I thought, would complement the white oak's brown well. And this is some lovely white oak. Not only does it have some cool ray fleck, but the grain has some funky glittery streaks, too.

I had planned to put some cocobolo pulls on the lids, but when I got to that point in the construction I just couldn't do it. No matter where I placed the pulls, they obscured the apple's beautiful grain and colors. So, I came up with a different way to remove the lids from the box. The box body was already finished, but that didn't deter me. At the drill press, I used a Forstner bit to create the finger openings. I actually used two different bits. The opening in the middle is slightly larger than the ones on the sides.

I don't remember when I decided to paint the top face of the box bottom. In the past, I've made fabric cushions for the insides of boxes, and I always choose a fabric that popped. That led to the milk paint, I guess. I just like the surprise of opening an all-wood box and seeing a bright splash of color. The marigold yellow milk paint looks great, and I like how it crackled of its own accord.

BOX 5 | 49

BOX 6

'veI made many boxes like this one before. It's actually my second go at a box I made many years ago. I made that box in one night, using a Phi ruler to determine the box's height, width, and length. I liked the width and length, but thought it was a little too tall. I always wanted to go back and make it again, but shorter. That's what Box 6 is. I should admit that I'm not positive that the two boxes have the same width and height. The only record I could find of the original box's dimensions was an approximation, so I guessed as best I could. (I gave the box to a family friend not long after I made it, so I can't measure it.) I like the proportions of the new box much better.

The first box was made from English elm. So is this one. The difference in color between the two is amazing. I really liked the color of the first box, but that board is long gone. I also like the English elm I used for this box, especially the random spots of wild grain, but it's not quite as nice. The top of the first box was solid wood. (I think it was flame birch—it came from a very old but decrepit table, so I don't know for sure.) The top of this one is plywood banded in cocobolo and then veneered with English brown oak. The pulls are cocobolo. The three woods complement each other well, and the darker oak works here because the box sides are a light brown. It would not have worked with the elm I used to make the previous box.

SPECS		
› English elm	› Cocobolo banding
› English brown oak veneer	› 1⅞ x 4 x 6½

ON IMPERFECTION

This box's pulls illustrate a strong belief I have about pulls and handles: Don't worry about getting them perfectly centered. If you look at the top right photo on p. 50, you can see that they are a bit closer to the right side than the left side. You notice this in the end view, but not when looking from above. I can live with some imperfection in a box, as long as it's in the right place. I suspect others will disagree with me on this point.

One of the things I look for when choosing wood for box sides is tight, straight grain. I also look for anomalies in the grain to give the sides some individuality. With cherry, it's usually bits of pitch. With this English elm it's some random, isolated curl or figure that makes the grain lines wave up and down. Very cool.

Box 6 wasn't hard to make, but it was tedious. Both the lids and the bottom involved veneering plywood. The banding on the top is mitered at the corners and getting those miters tight and clean was a slow, shaving-at-a-time process. The bottom involved some tedious labor, too. First I veneered the bottom face. Then I did the end banding. After that, it was the front and back. This way, when you look at the bottom from the front, you see what looks like a piece of solid wood. Last came the veneer for the top face. I wanted this to cover the banding, so that when you look at the inside of the box, you don't see any banding. The veneers on the lids are commercial, whereas those on the bottom are shopsawn.

BOXES 7&8

These two boxes are identical to the first two I made, except in the woods and paint colors. When I made those two boxes, I knew that I would come back to the design, because I like it so much and I wanted to experiment with other species for the boxes and different milk paints for the lids.

In this new pair, one of the boxes is made from riftsawn ash, has a pumpkin lid, and the pull is made from the wortled heartwood of a quizzical pear tree (actually, I made that wood up—I'm not sure what it is!). The other is quartersawn maple with a Lexington green lid. Its pull is apple. Of the two, I think I like the maple one better. The grain is so tight, and there's a bit of chatoyance to it. The green is also a great match for the maple and apple. But the ash has an earthy undertone that goes quite well with the pumpkin milk paint. The darker grain lines are a nice match with the milk paint, too. It's hard. I like both of these boxes. I suppose it's like choosing between your kids—on any given day you (might) like one more than the other, but you never stop loving either.

SPECS	BOX 7	BOX 8
	› Riftsawn ash	› Quartersawn maple
	› Pumpkin milk paint	› Apple
	› 1½ x 1¾ x 5	› Lexington green milk paint
		› 1½ x 1¾ x 5

BOX 7

BOX 8

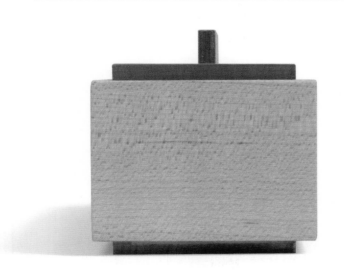

WHEN I USED LEXINGTON GREEN MILK PAINT FOR BOX 4, I CUT IT WITH SOME SNOW WHITE. THIS TIME I USED IT FULL STRENGTH. I'M GLAD I DID. THE DARKER GREEN WORKS BETTER WITH THE MAPLE. THE LIGHTER SHADE WORKS BETTER WITH WHITE OAK.

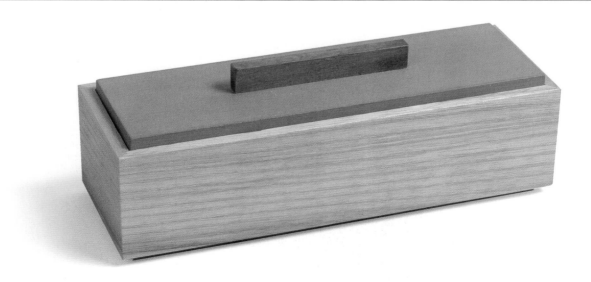

ON WOOD

Ash is one of my favorite woods, at least when it's quarter- or riftsawn. Back home in the South, all the ash I used was a beautiful creamy white with a hint of butter. Since I've been in Connecticut, I've bought locally grown and air-dried-by-me ash. I like the more earthy color it has. There's more to work with. Look at the nice brown streaks at the corner (see the bottom photo on the facing page). It allowed me to pull in the darker color of the pull. I love it. It's the kind of little detail that I geek out on when it comes to wood. Give me some funky little quirk and I'll build something around it.

There is one way (other than wood species and paint colors) that Boxes 7 and 8 are different than Boxes 1 and 2. Whereas the bottoms of the first two were natural wood on both faces, I painted the top face of the bottoms for these two new boxes (taking a cue from Box 5). It's a custom color I made by mixing marigold yellow and snow white. I like it. Once again, I got that cool crackle effect.

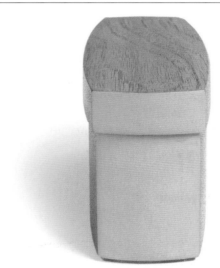

I USED BLUE PAINTER'S TAPE TO MASK
OFF THE SIDES. THIS MADE CRISP
LINES AT THE CORNER POSSIBLE, BUT
IT ALSO MEANT THAT THE PAINT BUILT
UP A SMALL LIP AT THE CORNERS. I
SANDED IT AWAY WITH SOME 320-GRIT
SANDPAPER BEFORE I SHELLACKED
THE WALNUT.

BOX 9

This box might look like others that I have made (walnut and marigold yellow together), but there is a huge difference between it and everything else I've made to this point. This is my first bandsawn box, and, let me make it clear, I really don't like bandsawn boxes. Here's why. The vast majority of the bandsawn boxes that I've seen are ugly. Very ugly. The reason they are ugly is simple. The folks who make them focus on the fact that they're making a box with a bandsaw, so they throw in all kinds of wacky curves, goofy shapes, and drawers within drawers. Technique drives the design, which is usually a bad thing. The box is meant to display the fact that it was made with a bandsaw. But who cares how something was made other than the person who made it? (I know other woodworkers do. We care too much about that sometimes.) Personally, I want the people who see my boxes not to even think about how I made it. I want them to say, "That's beautiful." So, I tried to make a beautiful bandsawn box. Perhaps I succeeded. Perhaps I didn't. I'll definitely try again.

SPECS	> Walnut
	> Marigold yellow milk paint
	> $2\frac{5}{16}$ x $1\frac{3}{4}$ x $6\frac{1}{4}$

OK, I'll get off my soapbox before I go too far. This box was a good learning experience. I've definitely thought of ways to improve the craftsmanship on my next bandsawn boxes. One of the things I figured out is that you get tighter glue lines if you don't sand the bandsawn surfaces after cutting them. Look at the top photo on p. 56 that shows the inside of the box. Those are machine marks left by the bandsaw. That could be a very cool surface texture on the inside. The next time I make a bandsawn box, I'll work on controlling the appearance of the machine marks. For example, for a fairly nuanced surface I could use a variable-pitch blade, like the 3-4 variable TPI resaw blades on the market. These blades are also very thin, and that would help with the glueline.

To create a shadow line around the bottom, I routed a very small (¹⁄₁₆ in. by ¹⁄₁₆ in.) rabbet around the perimeter. This is a small box (it's made from a piece of 8/4 air-dried walnut turned on edge), so that was an exciting process. Smart setup of the router table made it safe, but it was still exhilarating.

The lid's overhang is a natural consequence of the bandsawing process. The lid was cut from the body before the sides were cut free. Cutting the sides free removed material, making the box body narrower than the lid by the thickness of the two kerfs when it was glued back together. This is cool, I think. I exploited the technique for the purpose of design. (It was unexpected, but as soon as I recognized what had happened, I knew how I could use it.)

BOX 10

This is a little box, but it's big in terms of developing my design aesthetic. The body of the box is fairly standard for me. The lid is a whole other story. The pull, I'm sure, is the most obvious change for me. I've always done very simple pulls for boxes like this. Just a thin piece of wood glued to the top. This box is sporting a cherry pull elevated on little feet or stands that are painted with marigold yellow milk paint.

A less obvious deviation from my established design aesthetic is the cocobolo lid. First, I've used cocobolo for something other than a pull only once before. (I used it for the center drawer front on a bow-front cabinet I made for *Fine Woodworking* that was featured on the cover.) Exotics, I think, are too strong and dominant to be used for anything other than an accent. But this lid is causing me to rethink the role they can play in my furniture. When I was making this box, I really wasn't thinking cocobolo for the lid, but I stumbled across this piece in my box of cocobolo and ebony. It has strong, straight grain that's scaled perfectly for this box's proportions. And it had one face that was still rough from bandsawing. I thought the rough surface would look cool, so I left it. (I stole this idea from a box that my friend and colleague Mike Pekovich made.)

SPECS	› Cherry
	› Cocobolo
	› Marigold yellow milk paint
	› 1⅝ x 1¾ x 5

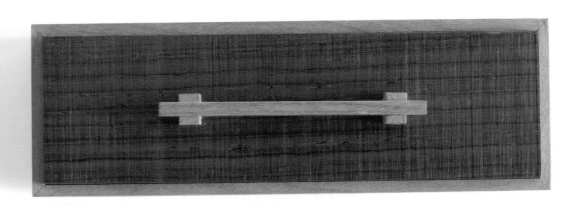

"*Thoughtful, good design begins with the overarching themes, but ends with the details.*"

This pull is an exercise in details. So, too, is the inside of the box. There's a wonderful little pitch pocket in the corner of the bottom that is visible when you take the top off. It creates just enough irregularity and breaks up the clean, straight grain of the cherry in a very nice way. When I'm picking wood to make a box, I'm always looking for straight grain with little spots of pitch, or curl, or a pin knot. Clean with some character: That's the ideal wood for me. Also, always pay attention to the details. Thoughtful, good design begins with the overarching themes, but ends with the details. If you forget them, then you haven't finished the design job.

To finish the lid, I just used some steel wool on the bandsawn face. I wanted to burnish, but not soften, the machine marks. Even a fine sandpaper would have rounded over the ridges too much. I finished it with shellac.

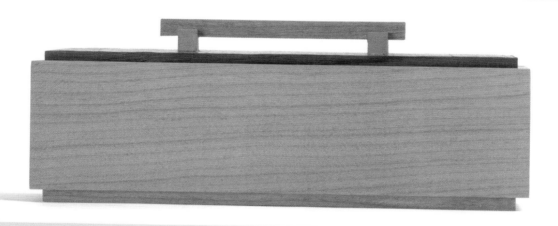

MAKING THE PULL

The little feet for the pull are sandwiches made from three layers of wood. The middle layer is actually cut from the same piece that the pull was cut from, guaranteeing that the "slot" for the pull would be exactly the right width. The two outside pieces are about $1/16$ in. thick. I painted the feet before gluing the pull into them.

I was worried that the irregular surface of the lid would prove to be a poor surface for gluing, so I attached the pull with stainless-steel brads, using the same technique employed with Box 1 (see p. 40).

BOX 10 | 61

BOX 11

I didn't actually choose to make this box. I made it because a jeweler I met really liked my smallest round boxes and thought they'd be a great way for someone to present the engagement and wedding rings she makes. Within a week of our discussing the possibility, she sold a ring to a client. So I had to make the box. I'm happy I did.

Here's a nice point about turning a box like this. You'll notice that the sides are not perfectly vertical. The box is actually slightly smaller in diameter at the top than at the bottom. The sides even roll in slightly at the top lip. If the sides were perfectly vertical, the box would have the illusion of being slightly wider at the top. Tapering the diameter ever so slightly makes it appear straight. It also makes it seem more delicate. And delicate is a good thing on little boxes.

| SPECS |
> Cherry
> Cocobolo
> Federal blue milk paint
> $1\frac{5}{8}$ x 2 diameter

The pull is a variation on a shape I use for every pull that I make, no matter what it's for. I love the shape. That asymmetric curve is lovely. Want to know how I came to it? It's the perfect shape to fit between my thumb and forefinger when I grasp a pull. The first time I turned the pull I kept working that arc until it was nice and comfy between my fingers. That's how I'd grasp a pull. If you grasp one differently, then you'd end up with a different shape to satisfy what's comfortable for that grip. This is a great lesson in how function and use determines form. If you do it right, then the form will be graceful.

The body of this box is made from 12/4 cherry that I bought off a former *Fine Woodworking* editor who was leaving Newtown, Conn. (where *FWW* is located) for the mountain west. I got quite a bit of it, and it's all wonderfully beautiful. I also bought my lathe from him. Thanks, Charlie! You made this box possible. And here's the lesson: Never pass up the opportunity to buy a beautiful piece or stack of wood. Never.

I'm very happy that this box will be used to hold an engagement ring. That's why I added the fabric cushion to the inside. That burst of color when you open the box makes the interior less dark. It's welcoming. But let's be real. The person who receives the box is justifiably going to be far more taken by the ring it holds. I thought about tying the box's purpose to Bilbo, Frodo, and the one ring, but even I have a sentimental side. May the happy couple be as blessed as King Elessar Telcontar and Arwen.

THE JOY OF MILK PAINT

One of the great charms of milk paint is how variable its color can be. The little batch I mixed up for Box 11 is much paler than other batches I've mixed. Look at the deep blue of the box body in the photo at right. That's a lot richer blue than the lid of this box. Still, both colors are great. Milk paint almost always looks great.

BOX 11 | 65

"You don't need to go to a strongly contrasting color to create variance. Do something subtle. Subtle is good."

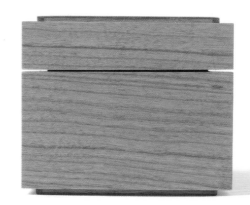

BOX 12

The proportions and general design of this box are strongly tied to the boxes that I've already made, but there are two new twists, and both work nicely. First, the entire interior is painted. The inside faces of the top and bottom are painted, but the inside faces of the box sides are not. Instead, I painted some liners and put those in after I cut the lid from the box. They are friction-fit rather than glued into the box and lid. I did this instead of painting the sides, because I wanted to use the liners to achieve the second new feature. Notice that there is a liner not only in the bottom (a common technique to keep the lid in place), but also in the top to create a small ($\frac{1}{16}$ in. wide) separation between the box body and lid. By adjusting the height of the liners in the lid, I could alter the width of the space between the box and lid. I like the dark shadow line it creates. I settled on $\frac{1}{16}$ in. because that's the width of the kerf cut by the bandsaw blade I used to do it. The grain flow from bottom to lid is natural this way. There's no discernible hiccup in the flow, as there would be if the lid sat directly on the box sides. Also, the top and bottom are both $\frac{1}{16}$ in. proud of the sides to mirror the shadow line between the lid and body.

| SPECS | > Cherry
> Marigold yellow milk paint
> 2 x 2¼ x 6

Now, back to the painted interior. I've wanted to do this for a long time, but this is the first box I felt it was suitable for. Perhaps it's not a surprise, but I like it. To do this successfully, the interior must be lighter than the exterior. Right now the cherry is still a bit reddish pink, but it will darken in time; the marigold yellow on the inside will stay just the same but pop all the more as the cherry darkens. It's really going to be eye catching in about a year. And, of course, marigold yellow milk paint has once again done me right. If only she could drink whiskey, dance to Van Morrison in the setting sun, and cook a mean low country boil.

The cherry veneer I used for the top and bottom is much darker than the cherry I used for the box and lid sides. Part of that is a function of age. I've had the veneer for at least 8 years. But it was dark when I got it, and it didn't change color when I scraped and sanded it. It is oxidized all the way through. You might think that's only possible because it's so thin, but I've cut into very old cherry boards that were completely oxidized throughout their thickness—and these were 1-in.-thick boards. Jointing, planing, and hand planing did not change the color. I hope the veneer is always darker than the sides. They complement each other nicely. And this can be applied more broadly. What's a great wood to pair with hard maple? Figured maple. A good wood for sapele? Ribbon-figured sapele. You don't need to go to a strongly contrasting color to create variance. Do something subtle. Subtle is good.

One more point: Look at the glorious little pitch knot on the front. It's not centered. It's just the right amount off-center. All by design. When I cut out the cherry for this box, I stared for a while, thinking about exactly where to cut it to get that pitch knot where I wanted it. I think I've said it before: There are no accidents in design. Be deliberate.

BOXES 13, 14, 15

'm not sure where to start with these three boxes. I could talk about the design, and I certainly will. However, in making these boxes I employed a technique that is quite brilliant (I developed it with significant help from Mike Pekovich). I guess I'll start with the design, as that will naturally lead to the technique. There is quite a bit going on with these little boxes (they're only just over 6 in. long), but it all started with a desire to make a box with sides that slope gently inward. I don't know the angle of the slope. I sketched it out on graph paper and went from there. But it is very slight. Because the sides slope inward, the miters at the corner are compound, and that's where the technique comes into play. I'll get to that in a bit.

I believe that a box needs to be lifted off the surface in some way. The way I normally do this is to have a bottom that is slightly proud ($\frac{1}{16}$ in. or $\frac{1}{8}$ in. depending on the size of the box) of the bottom edges of the sides. This lift creates a nice shadow line and gives the box a sense of lightness. With these three boxes, I decided to try something different. I cut a gentle curve into the bottom edge of the sides, creating "feet" at the corners.

| SPECS |

BOX 13
- Walnut
- Marigold yellow milk paint
- 2¼ x 2½ x 6½

BOX 14
- Cherry
- Lexington green milk paint
- 2¼ x 2½ x 6½

BOX 15
- White oak
- Marigold yellow milk paint
- 2¼ x 2½ x 6½

BOX 13

BOX 15

BOX 14

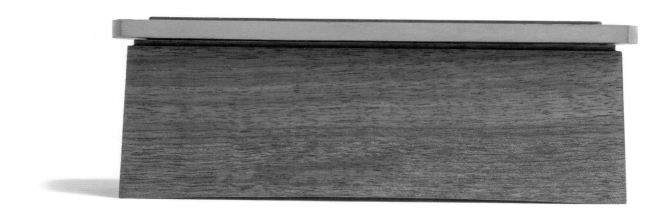

"Lift creates a nice shadow line and gives the box a sense of lightness."

The arc suggests that the box is lifted up off the surface. All of the arcs are ⅛ in. tall at their apex, but the ones on the ends look taller, because the radius of the arc is smaller than the radius of the arc on the front and back. I really like this technique for creating lift, and I'm sure it's one that I'll return to.

When I first sketched this box, the lid sat directly on top of the sides. It struck me as odd, as if the lid was a heavy slab holding down the box. I thought some separation would be nice, so I rabbeted the outside edge of the sides. The rabbet gives the tops a bit of float, and I really like the shadow line it creates. The tops have a shallow rabbet on their bottoms, which creates a raised field in the middle of the lid. This field fits into the box and that's how the lid stays in place. Because the box is rectangular, the sides of the field need to be straight. So, before I rounded the ends of the lid I cut the rabbets on the bottom. I then formed the round ends with a template and router bit. After the ends were arced I routed the rabbets on the top of the lid so that the field would be arced on the ends like the lid.

I decided to make the box in three different woods for several reasons, some having to do with experimenting with a new technique, but primarily so that I could try out different ways of using milk paint on the box. The walnut box has paint just around the edges of the lid. The cherry box has it only on the top field of the lid. (I like the Lexington green with cherry.) I used marigold yellow on the white oak box, too, but where it isn't immediately obvious. I painted the rabbet on the top edge of the sides. You can see it when you open the box, of if you get down low and view it from straight on. This box got the best reaction around the office at *Fine Woodworking*.

OK, enough about design. On to the technique. Compound miters are a pain to cut. Normally, you angle a miter gauge and then tilt the tablesaw blade to some angle other than 45 degrees. Because I worked on an article with Chris Gochnour, I know a technique for doing this that doesn't involve any math. It's a technique that Steve Brown from North Bennet Street School wrote about some 10 years before. It works, and I've used it, but I thought there might be a better way. So I went to Mike one day and threw some ideas at him. He came back with the wedge. He said that I should cut a wedge to match the slope of the sides, put it on a crosscut sled, and then tilt the blade to 45 degrees. The wedge would hold the sides at the correct angle to cut the compound miter. I immediately saw that it would work, and it did. The miters were absolutely perfect. And it was so easy. By the way, the wedge I made was actually longer than the front and back, so it supported the full length of the sides (see p. 74).

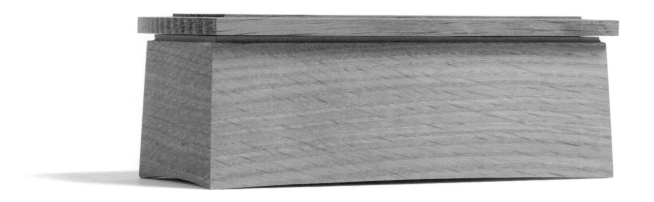

But I took the wedge even further. I realized that I could put the wedge in the routing templates for the arcs, and that when I routed the sides the bottoms would automatically be cut with the correct bevel on them. I also used the wedge when I ripped the sides to width, and that cut the top edge at the correct bevel. I even used the wedge to cut a groove for the bottom, and the rabbet on the top edge. Without the wedge, all of this would have been difficult. With the wedge it was dead simple. There was no fussing with the blade angle. For the miters it was at 45 degrees. For all of the other cuts it was square to the table. There was no hokey pokey with miter-gauge fences. I used my everyday box sled for all of the cuts. After I made the routing templates, I set a piece of the wedge stock into each one, and then put the box side on top of the wedge. Absolutely awesome.

WORKING THE WEDGE

1. Set the tablesaw blade at the desired angle and cut the wedge to match the slope of the sides.

2. With the wedge flat on the saw table, set the side on the wedge and cut the rabbet in the outside of the top edge.

3. Using the same technique, cut the groove for the bottom.

MAKING THE WEDGE

I laid out the slope on a piece of plywood, set a bevel gauge to the slope, and then used the gauge to angle my tablesaw blade. I then ran a long piece of poplar through the blade. It was wedge shaped across its width. This allowed me to cut short sections of wedge to use in the routing templates and on the crosscut sled.

4. Use the crosscut sled to miter the corners.

5. Put the wedge in the routing template to cut the arc in the bottom of the sides with the correct bevel.

BOX 16

This week I took another stab at a bandsawn box. I decided to stay with walnut and marigold yellow paint to have a connection to my first attempt (Box 9 on p. 56). It also has a similar shape, but because the blank was much wider I was able to give the sides a more pronounced curve. But this one is shorter, as it was made from a piece of 8/4 air-dried walnut, and I like the shape. The first one was made from a piece of 8/4 walnut (from the same board), but was turned on edge, so that the width (instead of the height) came from the 2-in. dimension. I took other design details from the earlier box. I rabbeted the bottom edge of the sides to give the box some lift off of the surface, and the lid overhangs the sides.

I also rabbeted the top edge of the sides, a detail I borrowed from the last three boxes that I made. And borrowing from the white oak version of those three boxes, I painted the top (and bottom) rabbet. I especially like this detail on the top edge, as it emphasizes the separation between the lid and box (see the top photo on p. 76). The milk paint continues on the inside of the box. I did not clean up the machine marks on the inside, so there is also a pleasing texture to the interior, and after I sanded the paint to smooth it, a bit of the walnut color peeked through. It's a nice touch.

I SPECS I

> Walnut
> Marigold yellow milk paint
> 1½ x 3⅛ x 6

As for the process of making a bandsawn box, I think I did better this time. I used the same technique but added a shopmade pivot fence, so that when I cut the sides free from the middle I could control their thickness more easily. I liked having the solid point of reference to work from.

BOX 16 | 77

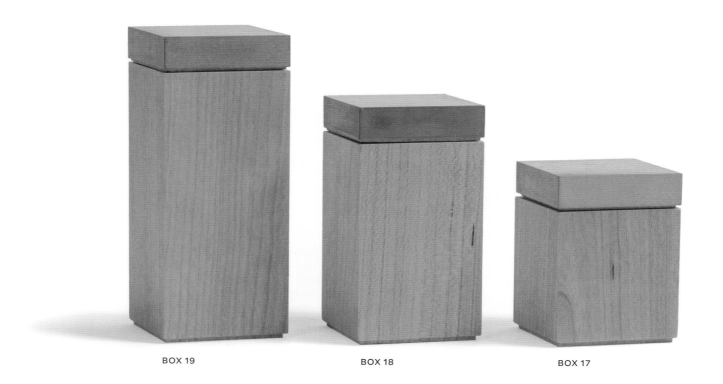

BOX 19   BOX 18   BOX 17

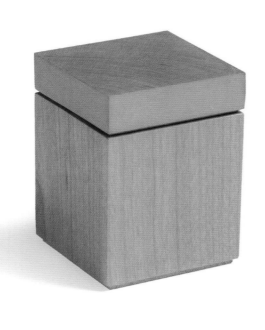

BOXES 17, 18, 19

made these three boxes because I asked myself a question while driving back from Maine. What's the easiest and quickest box I could make? The answer, I thought, would be to drill out the center of a block of wood. Because of the round interior, the lid would need a matching round "plug" to keep it in place. Turning this would be quick and not difficult. So, I started with a technique and the technique largely determined the design. This explains, I think, why the boxes have a mechanized or mass-produced feel to them. Normally, I design and then figure out how to make a box or piece of furniture. It results in work that has a far greater sense of having been made by a human hand.

I SPECS I

BOX 17
> Cherry
> Marigold yellow milk paint
> 1⅞ x 1⅞ x 2½

BOX 18
> Cherry
> Lexington green milk paint
> 1⅞ x 1⅞ x 3½

BOX 19
> Cherry
> Federal blue milk paint
> 1⅞ x 1⅞ x 4½

I used some 8/4 cherry for the boxes, and after milling the board square, planing the faces clean, and so on, the boxes ended up being about 1¾ in. square. I cut the bodies to length (2 in., 3 in., and 4 in. long), then chucked them into my lathe, where I drilled the holes with a 1½-in. Forstner bit. This works fine, but my bit was a bit dull, so the holes aren't as clean as I'd like. The lids were also made on the lathe. After turning the round rabbet that fits into the box, I cut them to length at my bandsaw. The visible thickness of the lid is about ½ in.

DRILLING OUT THE INTERIOR

1. Mount the box in the lathe chuck.

2. To drill the hole, advance a 1½-in. Forstner® bit into the end of the box.

3. Turn the lid "tenon" that fits into the inside of the box.

Here's what I like about the design. The best things about the boxes are their vertical orientation and the end grain on the tops. Using a piece of riftsawn cherry makes both work well. The straight grain running vertically on all four sides complements the design and also creates cool, diagonal end grain. I also like the bit of separation between the body and lid. It was created by rabbeting the lid after the round plug was turned.

As for the other side of the coin (what I don't like), I'm not sure that the painted edge of the lids works. Had the edge been thinner, it would look much better. Also, the round interior is not so great. (I wonder if my shop's hollow-chisel mortiser could hollow out the tallest of these boxes? I think I have some experimenting to do.)

BOX 20

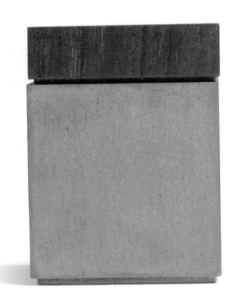

BOX 20

There were several boxes I could have chosen for Box 20, but I went with this one because of its link to the last three. I made the body for this one at the same time I made the other three, with the intention of painting it and using a lid from natural wood. Otherwise, it's the same as those three boxes. (It's the same size as the smallest of those three, about 2½ in. tall.)

The body is painted with a custom green milk paint that I mixed from Federal blue and marigold yellow milk paint. I really like it. In fact, it has earned a place alongside marigold yellow as my favorite. It is very close in color to a glaze used on a lot of Arts and Crafts pottery I have seen. I've even figured out a way to apply it with a brush that makes it look very much like a ceramics glaze. I know that many woodworkers would question why I'd want that. After all, don't we make things from wood because we love its natural beauty? Absolutely, but I've been fascinated with the amazing ceramics I've seen when teaching at Peters Valley School of Craft, and I've been working toward incorporating something akin to glazes in my work. This is especially true of my work at the lathe. I want to turn pottery on a lathe.

| SPECS |
> Cherry
> Walnut
> Custom green milk paint
> 1⅞ x 1⅞ x 2½

Part of what makes this box work, I think, is the narrow gap between the box and the lid. I've tried the box without the gap and it just doesn't look right. It helps that the bottom is rabbeted to create a shadow line. These two shadow lines create a nice symmetry.

I originally wanted to make a cocobolo lid for this box, but because of how I made it (turning a round lip to fit into the round cavity in the box), the lid began as a rather thick blank that could be chucked up in the lathe. I didn't have any cocobolo the right dimensions to do this. But I did have a lot of offcuts from some 8/4 air-dried walnut slabs. I knew that some of that walnut would have a nice, rich brown color when finished, so that's what I used. I like the color with the green paint. I also like the bold, straight grain visible on the top face of the lid. To make the walnut darker than it would be when finished only with shellac (my usual finish), I applied a coat of Waterlox® before the shellac.

DON'T BE AFRAID OF NEGATIVE SPACE. IT CAN BE USED TO EMPHASIZE THE STRUCTURE AND LINES OF A BOX TO GREAT EFFECT.

BOXES 21, 22, 23, 24

made this set of four boxes quite some time ago, but I didn't know what to do about pulls for the three small boxes up front, so they sat. I'm not crazy about the pulls I eventually turned for them, but at least the boxes are done now. If I were to turn them again, I think that I'd give them a more pronounced inward taper from top to bottom. The problem is that they are so small that it's hard to get too much shape on them without risking too narrow a diameter for the tenon and lower section of the pull. OK, enough about what I don't like.

The idea for this set of boxes has been beating about in my head for a long time. I decided on this particular arrangement because I knew that the boxes wouldn't be hard to make, leaving me to focus on the pedestals beneath them. For me, the pedestals are not just a place to put the boxes, but also a way to create negative space around the boxes. It's the particular arrangement of the boxes, including the shadow lines between them, that makes this set work. This meant that I needed to design them in such a way as to ensure that the boxes always maintain that negative space when the pedestals are fully loaded.

| SPECS |

BOX 21
> Cherry
> White pine
> Cocobolo
> 2 x 1¾ x 6

BOX 22
> Cherry
> Cocobolo
> Lexington green milk paint
> 1¾ x 1¾ x 2

BOX 23
> Cherry
> Cocobolo
> Marigold yellow milk paint
> 1¾ x 1¾ x 2

BOX 24
> Cherry
> Cocobolo
> Federal blue milk paint
> 1¾ x 1¾ x 2

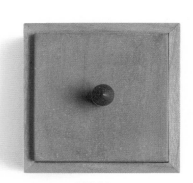

BOX 24

BOX 23

BOX 22

BOX 21

The four sides of the pedestal are made like a mitered box. The bottom fits into a rabbet, and the thin "top" into a groove cut into the sides. To create the defined recesses for the three square boxes, I fit dividers into dadoes cut into the front and back. These dividers also have grooves for the colored "tops." (By the way, the colored tops are just pieces of ⅛-in.-thick cherry painted with milk paint.) There was quite a bit of math involved in getting everything sized right so that the spaces between the boxes would be the same size and would put the outside ends of the first and third boxes in line with the ends of the long box in back. It also took some figuring to determine how thick the sides of the pedestals should be so that the boxes would be inset the amount I wanted.

I really like the proportions of the square boxes. I started designing the boxes by determining the width of the rectangular box, because I knew that the square boxes would have the same dimension. I then had to do some work to get three square boxes to fit into the length of the long box. In other words, I sketched out different lengths for the long box, trying out various widths of the spaces between the square boxes. Then I worked on the space between the rectangular box and the three square ones. After I figured out all the spacing, I turned to the pedestals. I think it all worked out well.

WORKING WITH COCOBOLO

All of the pulls are cocobolo, which is my favorite wood for pulls. But it's a cruel mistress. For flat pieces like the pull in the back, there always seems to be tearout because cocobolo tends to have annular rings that run in opposite directions (this is called "roey" grain). There's always some tearout that is hard to avoid, even with a card scraper. Oddly, it turns wonderfully and holds very crisp detail. It's not as good for turning as apple, though. Cocobolo has visible pores, which can affect detail (occasionally you get gaps in details because of the presence of a pore). Apple has no visible pores, so everything is crisp and continuous. Apple rocks. My favorite pie is apple pie, by the way. Blueberry is a close second. Mincemeat is a very distant last.

The recesses that hold the boxes are painted to match the lid of the box that fits into each one. For the rectangular box, which has a lid made from some very old white pine (salvaged from studs in my 100+ year old house), I mixed up a custom yellow that's close to the color of the pine. I like the little surprise you get from the colored recesses when you pick up one of the boxes. I brought these boxes into the office, and I heard several folks ooh and aah when lifting up the boxes. That's a great response, and it made me happy. And no one said a word about the turned pulls—as woodworkers we're always harder on ourselves than we should be.

The two pedestals are held together by some very thin and small spacers that are glued between them. I thought about a single pedestal, but not for long. I wanted to have some negative space between them and the best way to get a strong shadow line was to make two pedestals.

BOX 25

Box 25 is my take on a box made by *Fine Woodworking's* creative director, Mike Pekovich. I love the simplicity of having a bottomless box fit over a box with no top. I wish I'd thought of this first! Mike's box has a curly maple top—finished smooth with a nice luster—over an ebony bottom. He left the ebony rough on the outside (with milling marks from the bandsaw), just burnishing the surface with some steel wool. The contrast between the surface textures is fantastic. I've held this box and it's truly wonderful (see the top photo on p. 90).

My version of the box has an apple top and a hard maple bottom. Of course, there's a dash of milk paint, too. I painted the exterior of the maple bottom as well as the top face of the bottom panel. Only the inside faces and top edges of the maple were left natural. The bottom panel is plywood and glued into a rabbet. It's just a hair proud of the bottom sides, so that it sits just a smidgen off the surface. The top, I think, is gorgeous. The apple is amazing. I love the variegated color, and the green of the bottom is a perfect match. The top panel is plywood—like the bottom panel—and glued into a rabbet.

| SPECS |
> Apple
> Hard maple
> Custom green milk paint
> 2½ x 2½ x 4½

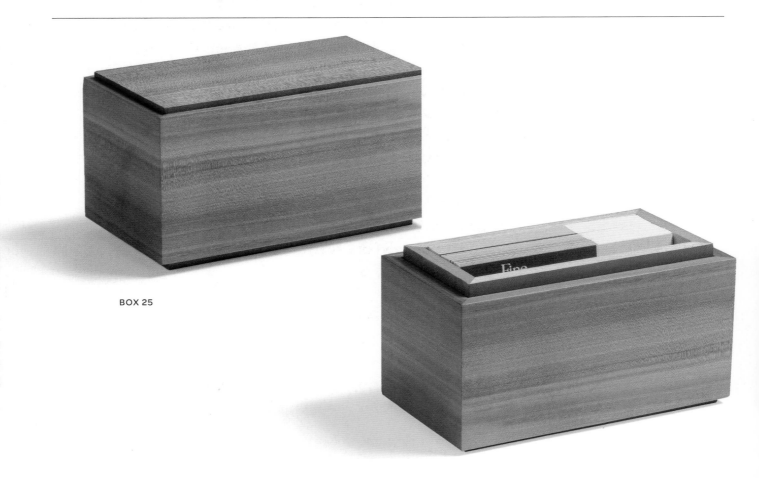

BOX 25

ODE TO MILK PAINT

Green, green, green. The loveliest milk paint I've seen. This is my new favorite color, a custom one I mix up using marigold yellow and Federal blue. This time I finished the paint with shellac and then wax (just like the rest of the box). The shellac gave the paint a slightly darker color that's a better match for the apple than it would have been if I used only wax over the paint (my normal process).

I did paint the inside surface and the edge of the top panel with the same green milk paint as the bottom. I like that little bit of green on the top box. It's a nice accent that picks up the bit of green that you can see when the top box is over the bottom one. The box is wonderfully minimalist…and modern in the best way.

As you can tell from the photos, the box was made to hold business cards. This is the second box of the 25 I've written about so far that was made for a specific purpose (Box 11 was made for a wedding ring). The box design works well for the purpose because you can flip the top box over and stick the bottom box back into it and have the cards ready for the taking. I made the box to carry my cards when I go on the road to demonstrate or teach. It's such a pain to carry a big stack of cards and keep them clean, neat, and tidy.

BOX 25 | 91

BOX 25

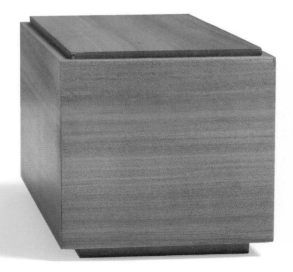

IN LOVE WITH APPLE

Just look at the color of the apple!
This could very well be the most
beautiful piece of wood I've had the
pleasure to use. I wish my photos
did it justice. I love the various
colors, different yet harmonious. I
could sing the praises of the apple
for hours, but I'll stop. Just look at it.
If it doesn't move you, inspire you,
then you should consider putting
your hand tools up on Craigslist®
or eBay®.

BOX 26

Well, let's get to Box 26, and we'll be halfway there. Although it's not immediately obvious, I used a peculiar technique to make this one. Take a look at the end of the box. That's end grain. Not surprising. This could be a bandsawn box. But it's not. It's a hollow-chisel mortiser box. I took a solid piece of ash, ripped off a slice to be the top, and then headed over to the mortiser. I then mortised out the inside of the box. This could be one of the smartest things I've done in the shop, or it could be one of the dumbest. I suppose I'll find out after a very dry Connecticut winter. If it stands up to severe contraction and then some spring expansion, I'll be happy. I think it will, but even if it doesn't it was still fun to make. It took all of 3 minutes to hollow out the box, and that's pretty cool.

I love the super-tight and straight grain on the sides. The end grain is good looking, too. Because the ash is almost perfectly quartersawn, the top and bottom are flatsawn. The bottom doesn't matter much, because you never see it, but the top is another story. I didn't want some ugly flatsawn grain messing up this box, so I decided to paint the top before I even cut it free from the blank. I didn't choose the color (Federal blue) until after I

SPECS	> Ash
	> Maple
	> Federal blue milk paint
	> $2\frac{5}{8}$ x $1\frac{7}{16}$ x $5\frac{1}{16}$

had hollowed out the box. I like the blue here because it stands out against the slightly brown creaminess of the ash. I also painted the underside of the top, so that the space between the top and box body would be more than just a shadow line.

Speaking of the top, I rabbeted around its bottom edge (the rabbet is the same size as the one around the box's bottom) to create the space between the top and box. I then glued a thin piece of maple to the underside of the top. This thin piece fits into the box and keeps the lid in place. As you can see, the underside of the top is also painted.

If you've used a hollow-chisel mortiser before, you know that the drill bit cuts a little deeper than the chisel. It leaves nasty drill bit marks. There was no way to get rid of them (without extensive and tedious chisel work), so I just cut a bottom from some thin maple, painted the top surface, and then put it in the box. I was going to glue it in place, but when I was testing the fit it got stuck, so I just forced it all the way down. If it falls out this winter, I'll glue it down.

BOX 26 | 95

"The connection is suggested, and a suggestion is often better than an explicit statement."

BOX 27

have mixed feelings about this box. I turned the bottom quite some time ago, and it was inspired by some Japanese tea cups that I'd seen. I love its shape. But then it needed a top. I like the top. I also like the pull. But when the pull is put on the top and top on the bottom, you get . . . an apple. And I don't like that at all. Of course, everyone who has seen it, held it, and opened it has loved it. Evidently, it would make a great sugar container for some tea drinkers I know. This is a case where I have to trust what those folks say. My dislike for the box comes from the fact that I had set out to make a box that gives a strong nod to some understated but undoubtedly gorgeous Japanese tea pottery I've seen. I ended up with a somewhat kitschy apple box.

Enough complaining. There is still a lot to like about this box. First, the lovely shape of the bottom. It fits my hands perfectly. Had I been a potter, this would be a wonderful tea cup. (Handles, as I understand it, are a bad thing on tea cups. If you can't hold it by wrapping your hands around a full tea cup, then the tea is too hot to drink. I don't drink tea—or coffee—but this is what I've been told.) The milk paint finish also is lovely. It's a home-made green that I made by mixing marigold yellow and Federal blue.

| SPECS |
> Maple
> Custom green milk paint
> Lexington green milk paint
> 4 x 3½ (dia.)

The "texture" in the finish comes from the brush strokes. There's a particular way to brush on the paint that leaves marks like this. To my eye, the finish looks very much like pottery glazing, which is the look I was after. The lid is straight Lexington green. To emphasize the difference between the two, I finished the lid with shellac and wax, whereas the body has only wax. Shellac darkens milk paint much more than wax alone. It complements the homebrew green quite well.

The curve of the lid is meant to pick up on the curve of the body, and the top of the pull is meant to bring the curve to a close. The three aren't exactly matched, but that's OK. The connection is suggested, and a suggestion is often better than an explicit statement.

I left the top rim of the bottom and its interior unfinished. I turned the bottom from hard maple. The stark creamy white is a nice surprise when you open the box. The pale rim is a nice way to separate the lid from the body. Eventually it will darken to the lovely honey gold that maple becomes, and that will be a nice touch, too.

BOX 28

This style of box has been around for ages. The ends are rabbeted into the front and back. The joints are reinforced with pins. A liner keeps the lid in place. While I have no particular fondness for the design, I was curious to see what I could do with these design details. Here is how I went about giving this well-traveled box design my own spin.

It started with the lumber selection. I decided to use some riftsawn sycamore for the body. I like the hint of warm, earthy brown underlying the overall lightness of the wood. Cherry might have worked for the pins, lid, and bottom, but it's a very rich color, especially after oxidizing for a year or so, and it would eventually be too strong for the sycamore. Instead, I went back to my favorite: apple. I had some shopsawn apple veneer that I knew would work for the top and bottom, and I just happened to have some apple pins sitting around, too. The apple's color is muted enough to complement rather than contrast with the sycamore, and the apple's variegated color is a good match for the multitude of hues in the sycamore. I sorted through the apple veneer and settled on this particular piece because of the small inclusion in the upper left corner and the three little knots in the lower right hand

SPECS	> Sycamore
	> Apple
	> Custom green milk paint
	> 3⅛ x 4¾ x 7½

corner. These imperfections add interest to an otherwise calm piece of apple. And that's important, because both the sycamore and the apple are subdued otherwise.

After picking the woods, I next thought about whether or not to use any milk paint. Just kidding. Of course I was going to use milk paint. The actual questions: what color and where? My home-cooked green is a great match for apple and I thought it would go nicely with the sycamore, too. On the outside, I wanted the apple lid and subtle shimmer of the sycamore to predominate, so I painted only the edges of the top and bottom. This is in keeping with my belief that you should use only three woods/colors on a piece: a primary wood to construct the box, a secondary wood for things like the lid or drawer fronts (there should be less of the secondary wood than the primary wood), and a tertiary wood for pulls or some other detail in very small amounts.

The inside of the box is a different story altogether. I like a nice pop of color when you open a box or cabinet, so I painted the inside faces of the top and bottom and the liner. The darkness of the green stands out nicely against the sycamore body. On reflection, the only thing I would have done differently is to not have painted the inside face of the bottom. Instead, I would have glued a nice piece of fabric down. I have some great light-green fabric with lovely little flowers (I am not ashamed that I think of things like this, and I like flowers) that would have been awesome in this box. Alas, I remembered too late. The bottom was already glued in place.

I also thought a bit about the box's size. I wanted to make something bigger than the ones I've been making. I like the proportions. It's about 7½ in. long and 4¾ in. wide. I think the sides are 3⅛ in. tall, and the top and bottom are about ⅛ in. proud. Proportions are always important.

RABBETING THE ENDS INTO THE FRONT AND BACK ALLOWED ME TO CUT THROUGH-RABBETS FOR THE TOP AND BOTTOM IN ALL FOUR SIDES. THE RABBET FOR THE ENDS IS AS DEEP AS THE RABBET FOR THE TOP AND BOTTOM, SO WHEN YOU ASSEMBLE THE BOX YOU DON'T SEE THE TOP AND BOTTOM RABBETS ON THE BOX'S ENDS.

BOX 28 | 101

*"The journey is as
much about the
aesthetics of what's
being made as about
how it's being made."*

BOX 29

Superficially, this box is almost exactly the same as Box 28. The obvious differences between them are the woods, milk paint colors, and pin shapes. But I think these differences make for two boxes that each has its own soul. A coworker at the magazine picked up on this right away. Box 28, she said, is feminine, while this box is its masculine counterpart. This distinction in their character can be explained, at least in part, by the choice of woods. The body of this box is mahogany. It's deep, rich color gives a sense of formality. The sycamore of Box 28, even though it has a lovely shimmer, is more gentle, more loving.

The beautiful curl of the figured top (and bottom) reinforces the box's formality, especially when compared to the earthy—and a bit carnal—warmth of the apple I used for Box 28. The apple is a late-autumn nap by the wood stove with a soft but somewhat saucy lady friend. The curly veneer on this box is a well-fitting suit and tie, a freshly shaven face, and an Old Fashioned in your hand.

SPECS	› Mahogany
	› Marigold yellow milk paint
	› 3⅛ x 4¾ x 7½

The shape of the pins also contributes to the difference in soul between the two boxes. Here, I've used ³⁄₁₆-in.-square mahogany plugs over some white oak pins. (The plugs are very shallow, about ¹⁄₁₆ in. deep.) Straight sides are harder than the softness of a circle (see photo below). Even the choice in milk paint colors emphasizes the difference in soul. Marigold yellow, which I've used on this box, is a strong, bold color, especially set against the mahogany. The green I used on Box 28 just doesn't strike the same tone. It's welcoming. It wants company, whereas the marigold yellow sings its independence.

What does this all mean? It points to the importance of choosing the correct woods, colors, and details for your work. Everything affects the overall character or soul of a piece: the color of the wood, the grain of the wood, the joinery, the size of the joinery, the choice of secondary and accent wood, the amount of secondary and accent wood (or paint), and a thousand other details to boot. This is the real work of a furniture maker. This is where you make or break a piece. And why it's more important to make something, then make another thing, then a third thing, and then a fourth than it is to worry about the tool you're using or the technique you used to cut a joint. That's how I see it anyway. For me, the journey is as much (no, more) about the aesthetics of what's being made as about how it's being made.

The mahogany I used for the box is, I think, Honduras mahogany, but I'm not sure, as I pulled the piece out of the scrap bin in the *Fine Woodworking* shop because it had excellent grain. I have no idea what species produced the veneer on the top and bottom. I was gifted a small flitch of the stuff by a coworker at the magazine. He told me the species at the time but I can't recall what it was. However, I do know that it's not mahogany.

"What does this all mean? It points to the importance of choosing the correct woods, colors, and details for your work."

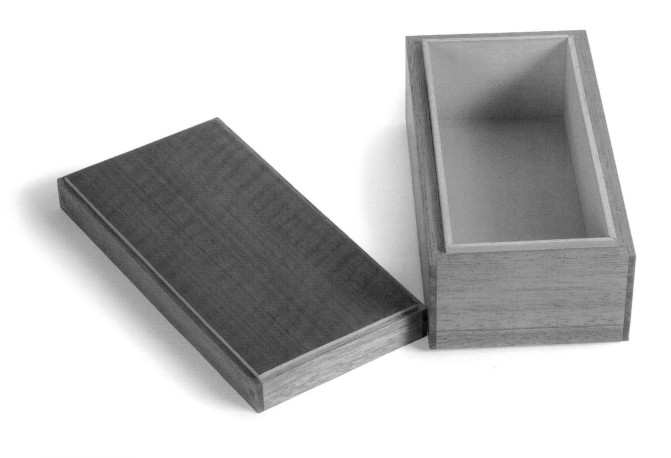

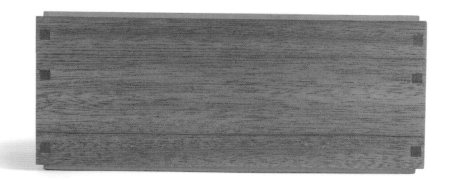

BOX 29 | 105

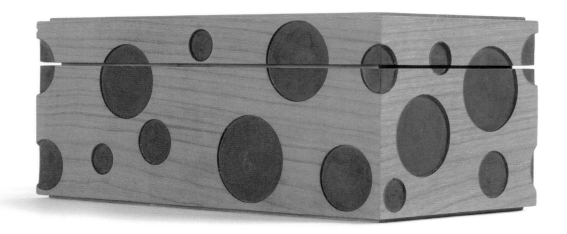

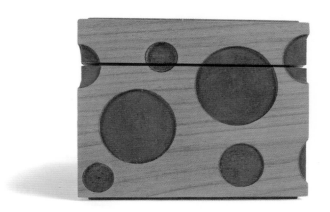

"Quiet grain is good, because it never fights against a box's design."

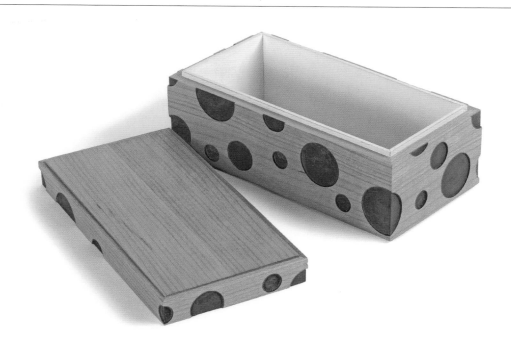

BOX 30

was tempted to run nothing but photographs of this box. The photos say more than enough about the box, but I figure at least a few of you will want to know what on earth I was thinking when I designed it. This is one of the first boxes I thought of after deciding to attempt 52 boxes in 52 weeks. Honestly, I don't recall where the idea came from. I think something like it has been bouncing about my brain for several years. I do know that it was boxes like this one that inspired me to undertake the challenge. All of the boxes I've made so far have been nice, but some of them really didn't push me aesthetically. I fell back into my comfort zone. This box is definitely not one of those.

What appeals to me about this box is how strong a graphic statement it makes. I love that the blue circles dominate the box. The riftsawn cherry I used for the sides is really just a background color. That's what I wanted. This box is about color and geometry. But note how the cherry's grain rises and falls with the larger circles. This symmetry between the grain and the pattern of the circles helps the grain disappear. Again, design is always in the details.

| SPECS |
- > Cherry
- > Light cream milk paint
- > Federal blue milk paint
- > 3⅛ x 4¾ x 7½

This also is why the top is made from some book-matched and riftsawn cherry. Keep the grain quiet. Don't distract from the sides. I thought about adding a few circles to the top, but I'm glad I didn't. That would have been too much.

The box took a long time to figure out and make because it is technically challenging. The blue circles you see are actually about $\frac{1}{16}$ in. deep. At first, I was going to drill through a thin, shop-sawn veneer, paint the underlying substrate, and then glue the veneer to the substrate. I thought and thought about how to do that and still get a good four-corner match. All the solutions I came up with were too fussy. I then moved to the idea of making a template and routing the circles into the sides. That's what I did, but I need to thank Mike Pekovich for helping me figure out exactly how to do it. After cutting the sides to length, I laid them out in order (front, side, back, side) between two fences and two stops at the ends. A long template fit over the top of the sides. I then routed the circles with my DeWalt® 611 with the plunge base. I used a ½-in.-diameter "dado clean out" bit from Whiteside. (It's the same bit I use with hinge mortise jigs.) This arrangement allowed me to wrap circles around the corners.

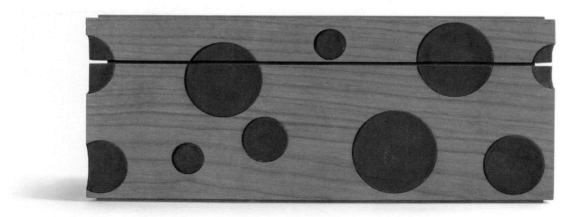

ROUTING THE CIRCLES

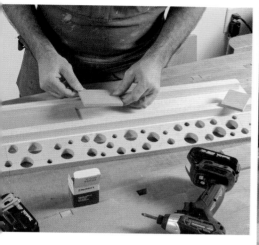

1. Lay out the sides and ends between two fences, butting the first side against the stop.

2. With all the pieces in place in the jig, screw down the second stop.

3. Use the template to set the depth of the router bit.

4. Put the template into the jig.

5. Rout the circles.

BOX 30 | 109

There's another important part of the design that also involves technique. Some of the circles bridge the bottom and top. I cut the top free at the bandsaw and then sanded the top and bottom on a piece of sandpaper stuck to my tablesaw to get rid of the machine marks. The cutting and sanding remove material and part of the circles. If the top sat directly on the bottom, you'd see a disruption in the circles' circumference. To overcome this, I used the box liner to raise the top and create a gap equal to the material removed. (Remember when I did this with Box 12 on p. 66? I was testing out the technique so that when I made this box, I'd have it figured out. I've been working on Box 30 for a long time.) I need to thank Mike for planting the seed for this in my mind. I come to him with a crazy idea and the beginnings of how to get it done, and he helps me get to a solid technique for doing it.

I don't know what else to say. The box is the same size as Boxes 28 and 29. The top and bottom are glued into rabbets. They're plywood—painted on the inside face and covered with shopsawn veneer on the outside. The liner is cherry, too, but painted with light cream milk paint from Old Fashioned Milk Paint. The blue for the circles is my old friend, Federal blue. One other thing: When my son saw this box, he saw Swiss cheese. Others have seen bubbles. Me? I see the one ring, which always sizes itself to fit the finger that wears it at the moment. But then again, I'm a bit of a dork.

BOX 31

This is a simple box. It's just a small piece of veneer, some quiet wood for the sides, and a bit of milk paint as an accent. But it's stunningly beautiful, primarily because of the balance struck between them. It certainly helps that the proportions are spot on—good bones are always beautiful. (It's less than 2 in. tall, 4 in. wide, and 8 in. long.) And the box is an excellent example of using woods (and colors) that complement rather than contrast with one another. Sometimes a plan comes together. And like Hannibal, I love it when that happens.

Let's start with the burl veneer I used on the top. I have no idea what species of wood it is. I was given three flitches of this veneer by a friend. The color is fantastic. So, too, is the figure. But what really makes this veneer work on this box is that the individual "burls" are small. It's super intense, but it's also well proportioned for a small box. Big, loose burl wouldn't have looked right. It would have been out of scale to the rest of the box, which would have disrupted the box's harmony. That might sound silly—or even overly precious—but when you design a box or a piece of furniture, you must give thought to every detail.

I SPECS I	› Madrone
	› Burl veneer
	› Custom green milk paint
	› 1¹⁄₁₆ x 4 x 8

WAITING FOR THE RIGHT BOX

The piece of madrone I used for the sides was small, an offcut from a wall cabinet I made years ago. It's been hanging out in the shop, waiting for the right box to come along. It finally did. It's wonderful how little pieces of wood, long forgot- ten, pop up from the depths of memory at just the right moment. And this piece did. I remembered everything about it: dimensions, color, and grain. Perhaps I grow too attached to the lumber I own.

I chose riftsawn madrone for the sides. I could have used cherry, but cherry has too much red and pink in it. I could have gone with walnut, but walnut is too dark for this veneer. Madrone is a finely grained wood with a lovely earthy brown sapwood. The grain on the piece I used was straight and tight. It's quiet—the perfect complement to the muscular burl on top. There can be only one dominant wood in any one piece. The others should serve to bolster its strength.

The green milk paint was easy to pick. The madrone is close enough in color and the fineness of its grain to apple that I knew that the green I used on Box 25 (see p. 89) would work well as an accent. Deciding to paint just the edges of the top (and bottom) was easy, too. I've done that before and it works well to separate the box sides from the top. Here, it emphasizes the shape and figure of the top. Figuring out what to do on the inside of the box was harder. At first, I was going to paint the bottom and the dividers (and have more dividers), but that seemed too busy for such an understated box. I eventually worked my way to a bottom made from plywood and shopsawn veneer (riftsawn madrone) and just two dividers painted green. By the way, in the past I would have joined the dividers to the sides with a bird's-mouth joint, but here I went with a simple dado. I gambled that painted dividers would look better with a squared end in a shallow dado. I think the gamble paid off. The joint emphasizes the distinct difference between the sides and dividers. In this case, that's a good thing.

BOX 31 | 113

DESIGN SYNTHESIS

Here's something that struck me after I'd completed the box: It was easy to design and even easier to build. That may sound arrogant, but let me explain why I say it. The design part was easy, because I was pulling together several design details that I knew worked: a top that's a bit proud of the sides (and has painted edges), and that slides over the bottom, tightly figured veneered set against riftsawn lumber, dividers used to create a cool geometric pattern. I've used all of the design details in this box before. I just put them together in a fresh way. This excites me, because it means that maybe, just maybe, I'm getting to the point where my design aesthetic has a well-defined grammar and vocabulary that can be relied upon to produce beautiful work. The danger is that I'll be lulled into an aesthetic slumber and get lazy with my designs, rehashing the same details over and over. I think I can avoid that, at least for now. The making was easy because I've done it all before. There are no new techniques here. I made the box quickly. I didn't have to figure anything out. I could just work. In fact, it took me longer to finish it (because of the paint).

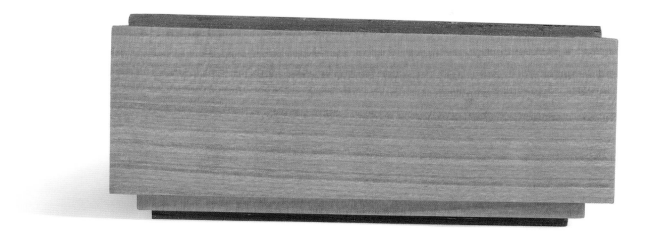

LESS IS MORE. THE INSIDE FACE OF THE TOP IS VENEERED WITH
THE SAME BURLY VENEER. I THOUGHT ABOUT PAINTING THIS
SURFACE, BUT I FIGURED THAT THE MILK PAINT WOULD HAVE A
STRONGER IMPACT IF I USED IT SPARINGLY.

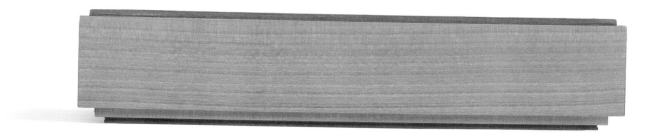

BOX 31 | 115

BOX 32

I suppose I should address the elephant on the wall first. Some might contest that this week I've not made a box. Here's what I say to this objection: I set the rules for this challenge and I decide what counts as a box! For me, this is a wall-mounted box designed to hold, keep safe, and display a sake set that belonged to my maternal grandparents. I can remember it in their house for as long as I can remember going to their house. My grandfather died first, and then my grandmother died little more than a year later. I went to their house after her funeral and was allowed to take this as a memento. I always liked it. I still do. If you look closely, you can see that a few of the cups were broken through the years and glued back together. I like that. The set meant something to my grandmother—enough that she kept gluing cups together—and so it means all the more to me.

I began thinking about how to display the carafe and five small cups, and went through a lot of ideas for the overall design before I settled on using a small box for each piece. I was drawn to individual boxes because it would allow me to arrange them in a nice geometric pattern (which I love) and to present each piece as something significant in itself. It then took several pages in the sketchbook to find the arrangement that I liked best. It's the one you see here. This left me with a bit of a problem: Why do I need that other long

| SPECS | > Douglas fir |
| | > Custom green milk paint |

box at the bottom? I'm not sure, but it balances the pattern well, so I stuck with it. I originally planned to put a drawer inside it, but the proportions aren't right for a drawer (the box isn't deep enough for one thing). Then, in a moment of opportunistic genius, I realized that I could put a box in there! Two birds, meet one stone. At the risk of spoiling the surprise even more, this smaller box that goes inside the box at the bottom will be Box 33.

My thinking next turned to how to make the boxes and the finer details. I wanted simplicity. The boxes are not what's on display here. A simple mitered box would fade into the background but provide an elegant frame around each piece. The back of the box, I knew, needed to be painted a light color to provide some luminescence inside the box and so that the sake set pieces would stand out against the back. Green can go nicely with brown, so I set about mixing up a custom green milk paint. This one is mixed from marigold yellow, Federal blue, and buttercream. The wood species fell into place after that. Douglas fir looks great with green and brown. Vertical-grain Douglas fir looks awesome on mitered boxes. The grain on the fir I used here is so tight and fine, that it's the perfect amount of subtle for the task at hand.

MISTAKES AS MILESTONES

You might notice a few darkish (greenish, really) stains here and there on the boxes. They're created when dust from steel wool mixes with the water in glue. (I finish the insides of my boxes before gluing them together.) I thought of removing these in Photoshop® but decided not to do it. Everyone makes mistakes and I tend not to hide mine. A mistake, Mike once told me, is just a milestone of your skill when you made a piece. Don't feel bad if you make mistakes. And for the love of Rosie Cotton, please stop pointing them out to everyone.

HERE'S THE RECIPE FOR THE GREEN. FIRST MIX EQUAL AMOUNTS OF THE YELLOW AND BLUE POWDER, THEN MIX THREE PARTS OF THE RESULTING GREEN WITH ONE PART BUTTERCREAM.

I USED FRENCH CLEATS TO HANG THESE BOXES. I INSET THE BACKS SO THAT THE CLEATS WOULD BE HIDDEN, BUT STILL A BIT PROUD OF THE BOX. I WANTED THE BOXES TO APPEAR TO BE FLOATING JUST OFF THE WALL. THIS CREATES A NICE SHADOW LINE AND LOOKS COOL, TOO.

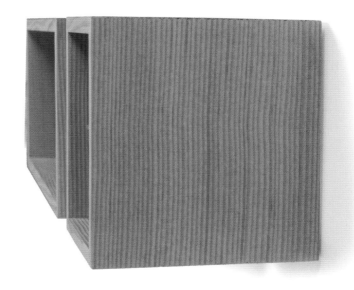

BOX 32 | 119

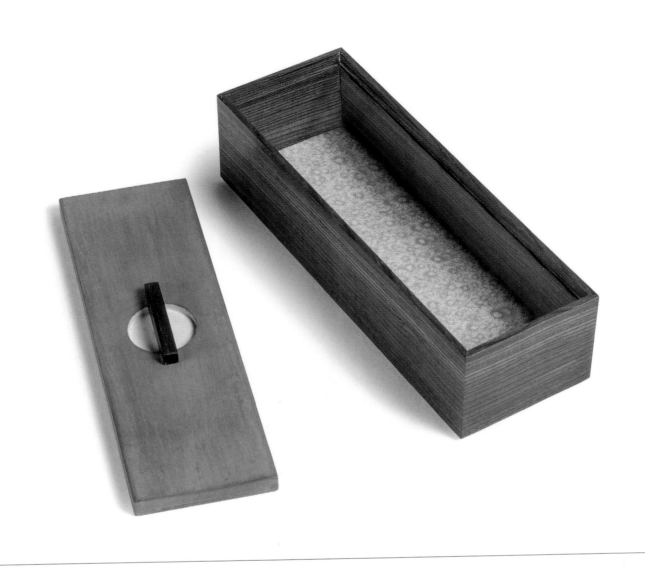

BOX 33

I made this box to fit inside the rectangular and horizontal box in the set of wall-hung display boxes in Box 32. The interior dimensions of that display box determined the dimensions of this box. I knew it was going to be a simple box with a top sitting in a rabbet and my standard bottom (plywood covered in shopsawn veneer and glued into a rabbet). But that's all I knew. There were important questions left to answer: What to do with the top? And what about the interior? And I had no idea what kind of pull I should use.

Before I could answer those questions I needed to figure out the box body first. I had the perfect piece of wood for it. A few summers back when I was working at the Lie-Nielsen® open house up in Maine, I began rummaging through the exotic woods for sale at the bench of Travis Knapp, who runs the eBay store RareWoodsUS. I found a 12-in.-long blank about 1¾ in. square. I didn't know what species it was, but the edge grain was amazing: beautiful, tight, straight grain. And the color was fantastic, too. Travis said it was kingwood. I bought it, went back to my bench, and planed that edge grain clean.

SPECS	
	› Kingwood
	› Ebony
	› Fabric
	› Lexington green milk paint
	› Snow white milk paint
	› 1¾ x 2 x 6

I fell in love. I'd been sitting on that piece, waiting for the right box to come along. This was the box. I knew that the wood's color would go great with the brown of the sake set. And the straight lines would complement the vertical-grain Douglas fir of the display boxes. I've never used an exotic wood for the body of a box—I prefer to save it for pulls and other small accents—but I'll have to try it again soon. If I can just find another piece of kingwood with grain like this!

Knowing that the box would sit inside one of the display boxes helped me figure out what to do with the top: Paint it green. I used Lexington green milk paint, knowing that a darker green would stand out against the light green I used for the backs of the display boxes. And the dark Lexington green would complement the rich brown of the kingwood. But the pull is really part of the top, and I had no idea what to do. So I made and finished the box, painted the lid, and then set the lid in the display box as it hung on a small piece of drywall (temporarily, for photography). Mike was looking with me and suggested drilling a hole through the top and painting the inside edge that was created. "Paint it white," he said, "because the inside of the sake set pieces is also white." Good idea, I thought. He then said, "Make it a little round scoop instead of a hole." I took that idea and ran with it.

The hole is shallow and has a flat bottom. I painted it with snow white milk paint. I then made a pull from ebony. The shape took a while. I fit the "tenon" part to the hole and then started shaping, putting the pull in place and taking a look, then going back to work on the shape. I like the final shape. It's low, so it doesn't overshadow the box, and the curve is very subtle. I shaped it all with a chisel and a rasp. And I really like the graphics of the rectangular green top with a white circle in the middle that's bisected by the thin rectangular ebony pull.

For the interior, I put into play a suggestion made to me by another *Fine Woodworking* colleague, John Tetreault (he's a great designer and furniture maker, too). We were discussing a group of 40 boxes (not part of this 52 box business) that I am making, and he suggested that instead of painting the interior face of the bottoms I should just glue some fabric to them. I liked the idea and decided to try it out here. I set the box over several different pieces (various colors, patterns, etc.) and settled on a piece that has brown flowers on it. It looks great. And gluing it to the bottom results in a much cleaner look than when I glue it to a thin foam pad. I'm fortunate to work with such great designers. I doubt I executed either Mike's or John's suggestion as they would have, but that's the way it should be.

LOOK AT THE FRONT OF THE
BOX AT THE RIGHT END,
WHERE THE COLOR MOVES
FROM DARK TO LIGHTER.
THERE'S A LITTLE BUMP IN
THE GRAIN AND THE COLOR
TRAVELS OVER IT. I LOVE THAT.

BOX 33 | 123

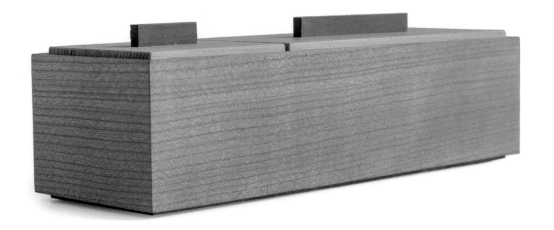

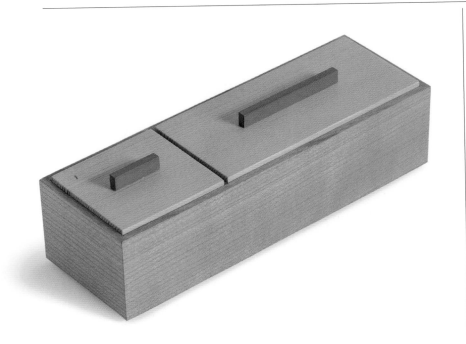

"*Good proportions are terribly important. Get them right and the box sings beautifully.*"

BOX 34

This box is similar to Box 33. They have the same dimensions, the bottoms were constructed in the same way, and both boxes have lids that sit inside a rabbet. But for all that similarity, they really are quite different. I made them both as an exercise to see if I could make two boxes with their own souls even though they had several important similarities. If I'm being honest, I'll admit that it was as I was designing this box that I realized a similar one would work nicely with Box 32, so I began designing this box and Box 33 in parallel. It was fun to make two boxes at the same time, using the same milling procedures, the same machinery setups, etc., and end up with two distinct boxes.

This version of the box actually sprung from Box 6 on p. 50, which in turn is a second take on a box I made several years ago (see the top photo on p.127). This time I went back to the original woods, cherry and white pine. It's a very good combination. This pine is some seriously old stuff that grew wickedly slow. It has super-tight grain and a beautiful, lustrous color. The white pine that you can buy at the lumberyard now bears a sad, pale semblance to the

| SPECS |
- Cherry
- White pine
- Custom green milk paint
- Fabric
- 1½ x 2 x 6

good old stuff. To match the tight grain of the white pine top, I used some cherry edge grain that also had very tight grain lines.

Although the woods are the same, I changed the dimensions dramatically. The original is 2 in. tall, 5 in. wide, and 8 in. long. I wanted this one to be small and more rectangular. It's about 1½ in. tall, 2 in. wide, and 6 in. long. The divider is 2 in. from one end. I know I've harped about the importance of proportions, so I'll go easy here, but good proportions are so terribly important. Get them wrong and the box is simply bad. Get them right and the box sings beautifully.

The original version of the box had cocobolo pulls. I didn't want to repeat that, so I went with painted pulls. I wanted them to be green, and I got lucky that I had some divider material left over from Box 31. I just ripped it to width, cut it to length, and then painted the ends. Perfect. I like the green with the cherry and pine. (I thought about painting the top edge of the divider, but decided against doing it. It's barely visible between the two lids, and the two pulls are enough color.) Another slight change from the original involves the fabric on the inside. Back then I glued fabric to some thin foam. This time I glued it to the bottom before I installed the bottom in the box. I really like the clean look of the fabric in this box. (I also used a different blue fabric. This one has a softer look.)

TAKE A LOOK AT THE SMALLER OF THE TWO LIDS. THERE'S A LITTLE MARK IN THE UPPER LEFT HAND CORNER. IT'S ACTUALLY THE REMNANTS OF A NAIL HOLE. I LOVE IT. THERE'S SOMETHING VERY APPEALING TO ME ABOUT HAVING A BEAUTIFULLY CLEAN SURFACE DISRUPTED BY A SMALL ABERRATION.

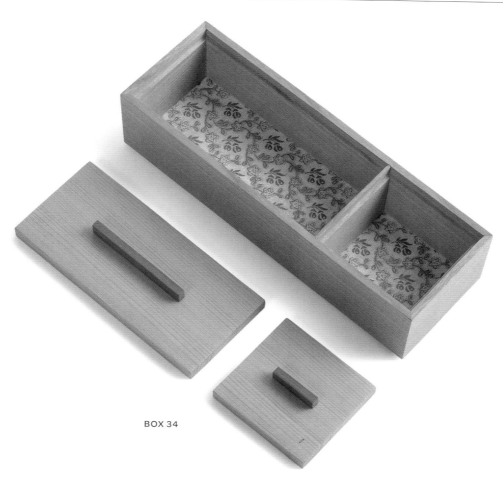

BOX 34

BOX 34 | 127

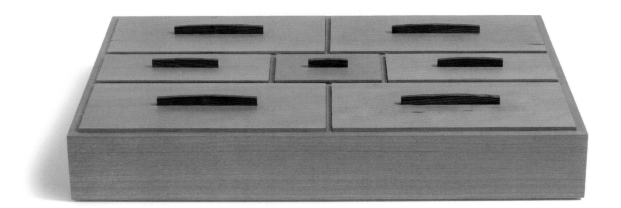

BOX 35

When I'm designing a box, the first three things I think about are the box's proportions, whether I'll be able to use the box's elements (lids, pulls, etc.) to create a geometric pattern, and how to incorporate a bit of color without overpowering the box. All three elements have a prominent role in Box 35. I'm not sure how I feel about the box, but the more I'm around it, the more I seem to like it.

This is the biggest box I've made so far: It's just over 12 in. long and 8 in. wide. The sides are 1¾ in. tall. It had to be this big to get so many compartments into it and still have them usable. I actually started out by determining the sizes of the individual compartment lids. I drew them out full scale, with the spaces between them, and that determined the overall dimensions. Of course, I could have adjusted the length and width of the lids to change the box's proportions had they not been good. I'm glad that I didn't need to do that.

| SPECS | > Cherry
> Kingwood
> Custom green milk paint
> Fabric
> 1¾ x 8¹³/₁₆ x 12⅝

However, figuring out that stuff came second in the design process. From the start this box was all about looking straight down at the lids, so I started by sketching out various patterns for them. I did this on a piece of graph paper with a ⅛-in. grid, so that I could draw a bunch of neat little scale patterns that are proportionally accurate. I don't worry about dimensions at this point. After I had the pattern and the proportions (for the big lids, it was 1 wide by 2 long—a nice proportion of width to length), I figured out the actual dimensions (going with 3 in. wide by 6 in. long). The spaces between the lids are just as important as the lids, so I spent some time figuring this out. The visible top edge of the sides is ¼ in. wide. The two long dividers that separate the three rows are ³⁄₁₆ in. wide on their top edge, and the dividers on each row are ⅛ in. wide on their top edge. The lids sit in ¹⁄₁₆-in. rabbets, so the sides are ⁵⁄₁₆ in. thick. The long dividers are also ⁵⁄₁₆ in. thick but have a rabbet on both sides. The short dividers are ¼ in. thick. The lids, plus the spaces between them, create a nice pattern.

The pulls also create a pattern. There are a couple things at play with the pattern created by the pulls. First, there's the placement of the pull on the lid. I centered them, knowing that this would create almost a rounded pattern. Second, there is the length of the pulls. Changing their length would change the look of the pattern. I think I did OK on this point. The pulls were actually the hardest part of this box. Initially, I was going to use rectilinear pulls, but they looked weird. Fortunately, I recalled the pull I made for Box 33. It's something of a stressed arc. I used that shape here, too. It greatly improves the look of the box over simple, straight top edges on the pulls. No matter how good you think something looks, always ask yourself what you could do differently and play around with the ideas that come to mind.

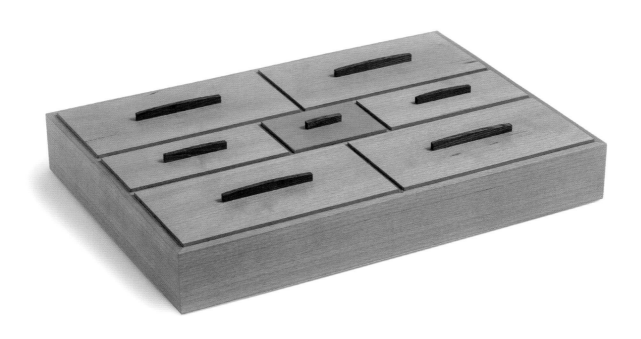

BOX 35 | 131

So, that's proportions and patterns. Let's talk colors. You've got the earthy, warm brown of the cherry. (All of the cherry came from a single board. It's the edge grain of a very old piece of 12/4 I bought from a former *FWW* editor, along with many other pieces of 12/4 cherry.) Then there's the rich brown of the kingwood pulls (made from material left over from the sides of Box 33). I knew that I wanted to paint the center lid. Picking the color wasn't tough. This particular green goes well with just about every wood I use. But that's not the only place I used it. I also used it on the edges of the other lids. This I thought was necessary to give some separation between the cherry lids and the cherry sides. It helps to emphasize the pattern created by the lids, too. The edge of the bottom is painted green, too, but you can't see it in any of these photos. The last bit of color is discovered when you open any of the compartments. I covered the bottom with a bold, blue fabric. I love how it jumps out, and adds a bit of brightness to the interior.

WOOD SELECTION

Originally, I wasn't going to make solid-wood cherry lids for this box. I was going to use veneer over plywood. I actually got a long way along that path, but abandoned it because I didn't like how any of the commercial veneers I have looked with the cherry, and the old-growth white pine that I have (I was going to cut it into veneers) was either too short or didn't have enough clean material between nasty defects, etc. I'm glad I went with the cherry. It has tight grain and a bit of curl, and because it's the same species as the sides, the patterns and proportions are allowed to take center stage.

BOX 36

This box came out of nowhere. As I was finishing Box 35, I was a bit frustrated because the quality of the workmanship is a bit lower than I'd like. There are a few gaps in the bird's-mouth joints. So, I decided to make a box and make it as perfect as I could. For some reason the first thing that popped into my head at this point was a very small ebony box. I thought that if I could come up with a good design and execute it perfectly, then ebony would make the box seem like a little jewel. I don't know if I accomplished my goal, but I really like this box.

For the most part it's a pretty normal box. It's 2 in. wide and 4 in. long, with sides that are 2 in. tall. The top and bottom have shopsawn ebony veneer on the outside faces and fabric on the inside faces. There's some shop-made poplar plywood between the ebony and fabric. The top and bottom are glued into rabbets cut into the sides. I glued up the sides, glued in the top and bottom, and then cut the lid free. And here's where the box takes an unexpected turn. A common approach to keeping this style of lid on its box is to use an insert on the inside of the box (I used this technique on Boxes 12, 28, 29, and 30). When I was designing this box, I decided not to use an

SPECS	> Ebony
	> Custom green milk paint
	> Fabric
	> 2 x 2 x 4

"Good design is always intentional."

insert. Instead, I thought that I might inlay some thin circles into the front and back of the box. The inlay would be glued into the lid, but not the box, so you could pull the top off, but when the top was on, the inlaid circle would lock into the half-circle mortise in the box bottom and keep the lid in place. I considered several other shapes, too. But, honestly, all of that seemed like a colossal pain to make. So, I thought some more about it.

Here's what I came up with, and it wasn't hard to do. After cutting the lid free and cleaning up the sawn edges of the lid and box, I routed a small rabbet into the lid and box. I then made some strips of maple that were just wider than the "groove" created when I put the lid on the box. I also left the maple a bit thicker than the groove was deep, so that it was just a few hairs proud of the ebony. My plan was to paint the maple, then glue it into the rabbet in the lid. That's what I did. The green strips are mitered at the corners. The strips automatically fit into the rabbet in the bottom and hold the lid on the box.

There's not much else to say about this box, but I do want to explain why I painted the strips that hold the lid on the bottom. I thought about using solid wood and quickly ran through the species I have on hand, like cherry, walnut, apple, mahogany, madrone, white oak, maple, holly, etc. None of them was the right color. And then there's the issue of grain. Ebony's grain is so difficult to see that even a wood with very little grain, like madrone or apple, looks odd against it. I also thought about using curly maple, which can look great with ebony, but the strips are so small that I feared the maple would no longer look curly. Also, ebony is so lacking in variation of color that other woods look odd juxtaposed against it when ebony is the primary wood. So, I decided to go with milk paint. It shouldn't be a surprise that I think it looks great.

One last point about the strips. I left them proud of the ebony for a few different reasons. First, I wanted there to be a tactile indication of how the lid comes off. When you put your fingers on the lid, you feel the strips slightly and can grasp them to help pull off the lid. Second, it would be damn near impossible to get them truly flush with the ebony. Normally, you'd glue them in place and then plane them flush, but I couldn't do that because it would remove the paint. Of course,

BOX 36   135

you could remove material from the inside face until the outside was flush, but because a bit of the inside face is exposed and painted, I couldn't do that, either. A third option would be to plane the strips flush to the ebony before I painted them, but then they would no longer be flush after I painted them and you would feel that. So, I intentionally made them proud, and they're proud enough that it's clearly intentional. Good design is always intentional.

LIFTING THE LID

1 & 2. Rout a rabbet into the outside edge of the box and the lid.

3. Cut strips of maple for the lid rabbet and miter the ends on a tiny miter shooting board.

4. Glue the first strip into the lid rabbet.

5. Fit the last strip into place.

BOX 36 | 137

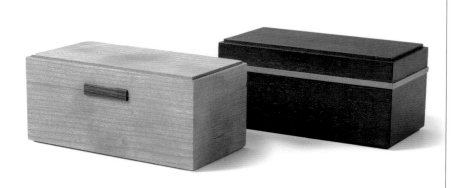

"It's important that all the details of a box be appropriately proportioned to harmonize with the box's proportions."

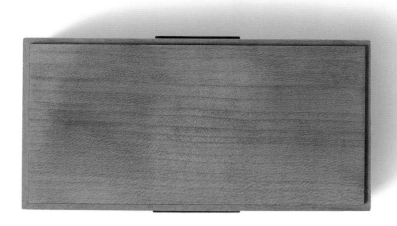

BOX 37

I made Box 37 at the same time I was making Box 36. They have the same dimensions and were made with the same construction techniques, but they clearly are not the same box. I like each of them individually, but I think they're better off as a pair. The underlying familial connection makes their individual beauty shine even brighter. When I first got the notion of making 52 boxes in 52 weeks, I envisioned making individual boxes, but I've grown fond of building a pair of boxes around a few basic design ideas (proportions, use of color, etc.), taking each box in a different direction while letting their bones tie them together quietly. I wonder how many boxes I could do this with. I think three would work nicely. More than that and perhaps the magic is gone.

This box is cherry, with kingwood pulls. It's a great pairing. Kingwood is in the same genus *(Dalbergia)* as cocobolo, rosewood, and African blackwood, so it's no surprise that it complements cherry so well. The pulls are mortised into the lid. I cut a matching mortise in the box for each pull. When the lid is on the box, the pulls register in the box's mortises and hold the lid in place. It's simple and clean. I like it.

SPECS	› Cherry
	› Kingwood
	› Fabric
	› 2 x 2 x 4

I CUT THE MORTISES FOR
THE PULLS BY HAND. I LAID
THEM OUT IN PENCIL, CUT
THEM IN WITH A MARKING
KNIFE AND CUTTING
GAUGE, AND THEN USED
CHISELS TO CAREFULLY
PARE AWAY THE WASTE.
I THEN FIT THE PULLS TO
THE MORTISES.

Because this box is so small (2 in. tall by 2 in. wide by 4 in. long) it was critical that I pick the right piece of cherry for the sides. It needed to be riftsawn, with straight, tight grain. The grain on the piece I used is proportioned perfectly for the box's size. I think that matching the grain's proportion to the box's is something that many woodworkers do not think about, which is a shame. Let's say you make this box from curly maple—and I think it would look good in curly maple—the curl would need to be very tight so that you get a lot of little ripples across the sides. This makes the little box look like it was made from curly maple. Big, rolling curls just wouldn't have the same pop. The box might look splotchy or vaguely figured as a result.

IN THE DETAILS

Cherry goes well with blue, so I pulled out my blue fabrics. But the visible area of the bottom and lid are quite small. A fabric with a large pattern would look odd, so I went for one that has a small flower (in blue) all over it. It gives the sense that the fabric was made for a box just this size. A big pattern would suggest that I used a fabric meant for something big, like a quilt, and crammed it into this little box. Perhaps I'm odd for thinking about the fabric I use in this way, but I really do believe it's important that all the details of a box be appropriately proportioned to harmonize with the box's proportions (this is also true of all furniture—no matter the size). And my attention to this particular detail is only an example of the level of attention one must pay to the details when designing. Everything must be considered.

BOX 37 | 141

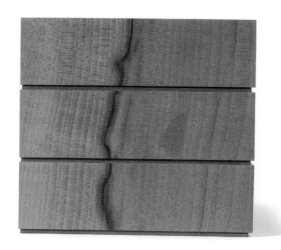

"*Design is evolutionary, not revolutionary. And it's certainly not ex nihilo.*"

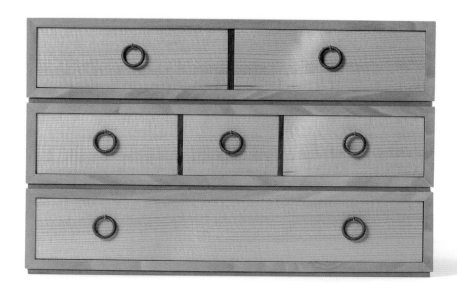

BOX 38

Box 38 took a long time to make, at least compared to the first 37. From beginning to end, I spent two weeks on it. Why so long? Six little dovetailed drawers with seven little ring pulls. And let me not forget the drawer bottoms. Those ate up some time, too. I'll get to the drawers later, but I want to start with the box as a whole.

What we have here is three separate boxes that are connected by some thin (1/8 in. thick) spacers. The boxes are made from a piece of madrone, and the grain runs up the side, over the top, then back down the other side. It's a dramatic piece of madrone, as it has both sapwood and heartwood. The sapwood, which is a bit lighter in color and on the front of the cabinet, is separated from the heartwood by a dark undulating streak. It's an amazing and striking graphic. This streak is critical to the design's success. It holds the three boxes together, even though they're separated by small gaps. There's no denying that this particular piece of madrone is spectacular. (And woe is me, because I've now used up all of my madrone. All that's left are offcuts. Perhaps there's enough for a little box.)

| SPECS |
> Madrone
> White pine
> Custom green milk paint
> Thread
> 6⅜ x 6¾ x 10

The madrone's phenomenal beauty actually made it difficult to make the drawers. The fronts are old-growth quartersawn white pine. However, these are the second fronts the drawers have had. The first set of fronts were madrone, cut from the same board as the boxes. The dark streak ran down the center of the middle row of drawers. But its horizontal run was in such tension with the streak on the boxes, that I cut those fronts off almost completely (I kept the dovetail joinery) and then glued on the white pine veneers that you see. They're thick for veneers, between $1/32$ in. and $1/16$ in. thick. The tight and subdued grain of the white pine works much better with the grain on the boxes. The fronts are really just a nicely contrasting color with a hint of grain. It helps that the grain lines are reddish-brown, which connects the fronts to the earthy browns and reds of the madrone. So, instead of a strong, visual grain fighting against the grain of the boxes, there's just a lovely, warm honey-colored bank of drawer fronts.

Viewed from the front, the drawers create a pleasing geometric pattern that's nicely accentuated by the ring pulls. I made the pulls from small metal rings, wrapping them in a thick thread that's a shade of green much darker (and closer to true green) than the milk-painted spacers. The pulls hang from small brass cotter pins. These are, in essence, the same pulls that I used on Box 4 (see p. 44), but I didn't use hemp twine, because I thought the twine's color and coarseness weren't suitable for this box. The pulls aren't the only similarity between Boxes 38 and 4. I used a walnut divider on Box 4. This time it's cocobolo, but I set the divider back $1/16$ in. and the drawers are flush with it. The divider on Box 4 is flush with the front edge of the box and only the drawers are inset. Also, the idea for Box 38 came from wondering what Box 4 would look like if I stacked two more on top of the original. Design is evolutionary, not revolutionary. And it's certainly not ex nihilo.

WOOD WORDS

In no particular order, here are my five favorite species of wood (at least right now): madrone, riftsawn cherry (I don't like quartersawn), apple, vertical-grain Douglas fir, and old-growth quartersawn Eastern white pine. I love that I've gotten to the point where I'm this finicky about wood. New-growth quartersawn Eastern white pine? Forget about it. The old stuff has a color, tightness of grain, and luster that's intoxicating, and it's so unlike the new stuff that, at least from the perspective of a furniture maker, they might as well be two separate species. I'm fortunate to live in New England, where old studs and timber frames yield this beauty from time to time.

BOX 38 | 145

ATTACHING THE SPACERS

1. The spacers between the boxes are made from strips of basswood painted with milk paint. First, glue and clamp the mitered front strip.

2. Glue down the side spacers, which are mitered to join the front strip.

3. The back spacer fits between the two side ones (butt joint) and is inset a bit, so that even if the box expands, it won't ever stick out past the back end of the side spacers.

THE FRONT AND BACK SPACER STRIPS RUN WITH THE GRAIN. THEY'RE GLUED DOWN COMPLETELY. THE SIDE SPACERS ARE GLUED AT THE FRONT, TO THE BOX ABOVE THEM, BUT NOT AT ALL TO THE BOX BENEATH THEM. THIS ALLOWS FOR WOOD MOVEMENT.

Back when I was making Box 4, I ripped some nice walnut to create narrow strips with very straight grain. They came from the edge, rather than the face, of a board. I did the same here. I ripped several thin strips from a piece of white pine to turn the edge grain into face grain. I glued them up into a panel and planed them to fit into the drawer bottom groove. So, the bottom is just ⅛ in. thick. That's plenty thick for a little box like this, as long as you don't store your Pee Paw's coin collection in the drawers. I love the tight, straight grain of the bottoms. It's just as important to be beautiful on the inside as on the outside.

BOX 39

When I began thinking about making a kindling box (actually mine is a box for fatwood), I was thinking of having the opening on top but using a lid on hinges so that it would be neat and tidy—in keeping with my overall preference for clean lines. However, something about that struck me as odd, and I don't really know why, but I thought to myself, just turn it onto its side. The fatwood I use to start my wood stove is of a uniform length and can be stacked easily, so I knew it would work.

I thought that a box open on one side with a bunch of kindling stacked in it would look a bit strange, so I decided to add a drawer to hold matches, a lighter, or anything else you might need to start a fire. Putting the drawer at the bottom would create some shape to the interior, especially with the kindling stacked up the side and over the top of the box compartment. I really like the way it looks.

| SPECS |
> White pine
> Apple
> Thread
> 15½ x 11½ x 20

BOX 39 | 149

I next thought about the joinery, and a base. For quite some time I've wanted to make a box with through-mortise-and-tenon joinery, where the tenons were sized and spaced in a way similar to how I size and space dovetails. Running the sides up past the top allowed me to use the joinery for the top. If you did this at the end of a board, the mortises would be too weak. (Running the sides and back up past the top also created a cool little gallery.) I was unsure what to do at the bottom of the box. I could have run the sides down past the bottom, allowing me to use the through-tenons again and to create feet, but I thought that the box would look too traditional, and I wanted something modern. So, I split the base off from the box and used through-dovetails on both. The size and spacing of the tails mirrors the size and spacing of the tenons. I deliberately chose to put the tails on the horizontal boards so that you'd see their end grain when looking at the sides, just as you see the tenons' end grain. I also ran the grain continuously up the sides from the base to the box. It helps tie the two together. To space the box and base, I used three small bars that are as thick and wide as the other parts are thick.

The drawer front is apple. The other drawer parts are white pine (just like the box). I thought about painting the front with milk paint, but this piece of apple was exactly the right thickness and width for the front, and I knew that the apple would look great with the white pine. For the pull, I stacked two metal rings, one in front of the other, and then wrapped them with a thick brown thread. The pull hangs on a stainless-steel cotter pin. I love it.

Finally, the back. I wanted to use a frame-and-panel back to control wood movement. It also allowed me to glue the back in place, which is important because screwing it in place really wasn't an option. However, I did use three nails to secure it to the top. I used glue on the sides and bottom. But anyway, back to what's really cool about the back. It has the standard two rails and two stiles, but I decided to try out something that I've seen Clark Kellogg use, so I added two pieces to the frame and these follow the contour of the drawer compartment. It looks awesome and wasn't hard to do. Thanks, Clark.

BOX 40

When I first set out on this adventure in box making, I explicitly had it in mind that there would be some boxes that I would make more than once, so that I could explore the design and hopefully improve it with each iteration. Box 40 is one of these boxes. It is the same as Boxes 1, 2, 7, and 8. There are a few subtle differences, of course. First, Box 40 is made from apple. As you know by now, it's one of my favorite woods, and I had a small piece that was just big enough for the sides and bottom of this box. The lid is painted with milk paint, like those other boxes, but it's a different color. This green is my favorite color of milk paint, and it looks great with apple. Third, the interior is finished with a bit of fabric glued to the bottom. Finally (and this is the true reason I took a fifth stab at this box), I used a new style of pull. It's the same pull I used on the biggest lids on Box 35 (see p. 128). When I made it for that box, I thought it might look good on other boxes that I've made, so I made a box to test out that theory.

| SPECS | › Apple |
| › Kingwood/cocobolo |
| › Custom green milk paint |
| › Fabric |
| › 1½ x 1¾ x 5 |

"That's all creativity really is. It's simply a matter of answering the question, 'What can I do differently?'"

I think this new pull is a big improvement (though I'm not sure if it's kingwood or cocobolo), bringing the box to a higher level of refinement and one step closer to being a fully resolved design. The previous pull for this box was just a stick. Honestly, it was a stick because I didn't know what else to do. It wasn't until Box 35 that I begin to think differently about the pull. That's all creativity really is. It's simply a matter of answering the question, "What can I do differently?" (I learned that lesson from Hank Gilpin.)

Actually, this box might now be fully resolved, but I could always try out some other pull shapes and interior treatments. In fact, the pull might be slightly better if it were a stressed curve. Just a bit of rounding off rather than coming to a peak, and it would be quite nice. This is exciting for me. Sure, this box isn't as sexy as the last two, but it feels great to see a design evolve and get better.

Just 12 more boxes to go now! I have a few of them planned, but otherwise it's wide open. That's a bit scary. It's also very exciting. I know that I'll get all 52 done, so there's an element of surprise about what's to come. I can't wait to see what I pull out of the proverbial hat. (I do know that there will not be a rabbit-shaped box, so don't worry about that.)

BOX 40 | 153

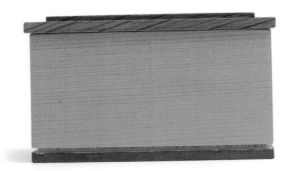

"Tight, straight grain emphasizes rather than fights the small box's lines."

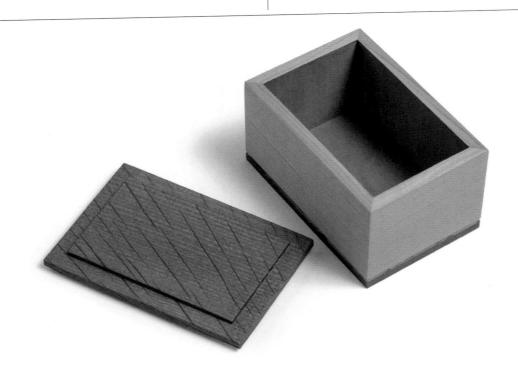

BOX 41

This is a little sugar box. The sides are made from salvaged, old-growth white pine that's quartersawn. The grain is very fine, tight, and straight, which makes it just right for a box this small. However, it presented a problem when it came time to pick a piece of wood for the lid. I didn't have a species in mind, really. I was more concerned with finding something with tight, straight grain. I found what I wanted in a small white oak board. It's quartersawn, which might have been a problem had the ray fleck been wild or large. Luckily, the flecks are narrow and straight, running diagonally across the grain. I love the look.

I was fortunate to have both white pine and oak with grain proportionally well suited for this little box. Grain spaced more widely, or flatsawn grain, would make for a less delicate and elegant box.

| SPECS |
- White pine
- White oak
- Custom green milk paint
- $1\frac{7}{8}$ x $2\frac{1}{8}$ x $3\frac{1}{8}$

Having chosen wood for the sides and lid, I turned my thought to milk paint. The custom green paint that I've used in the past goes very well with white pine and white oak, so I settled on this color fairly quickly. How to use it was another question. Because the box is so small, I didn't want too much paint on the outside, and I didn't want to paint any part of the sides—the grain is just too beautiful to paint over. So, I thought about the bottom and realized that I had an opportunity to use a style of bottom that I've had in mind for a while but not used yet. I normally use the bottom as a way to create some separation between the box and the surface that it sits on, and because the bottom is inset from the outside faces of the sides, a narrow shadow line is created. This gives the box a lighter and more delicate appearance. The bottom of this box was not made like that. It's more like a little pedestal for the box to sit on.

I glued some shopsawn veneer (from the same piece of pine as the sides) to a very thin piece of plywood. I then rabbeted around its top face. After gluing the bottom to the box (this is why I went with a laminated bottom rather than a solid-wood one), a small groove was created to give some separation between the box and bottom. And because the bottom is so thin, the bit of edge left was just the right size to be painted without becoming overbearing. I'm pleased with how it turned out.

The lid is rabbeted on the top and bottom. The field created by the rabbets on the bottom fits into the box and keeps the lid on. The lid overhangs the sides about ¹⁄₁₆ in. so that you can get a hold of it to take it off.

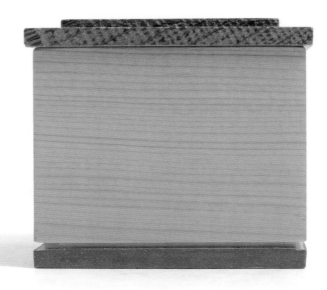

I PAINTED THE INTERIOR FOR TWO REASONS. FIRST, MILK PAINT IS NONTOXIC, SO IT'S A GREAT FINISH FOR SOMETHING THAT WILL TOUCH FOOD. SECOND, I LIKED THE IDEA OF HAVING THE WHITE SUGAR (OR EVEN THAT BROWN, COARSE SUGAR) SET AGAINST A DARKER COLOR. WHEN YOU OPEN THE BOX, YOU GET A NICE LITTLE POP.

BOX 41   157

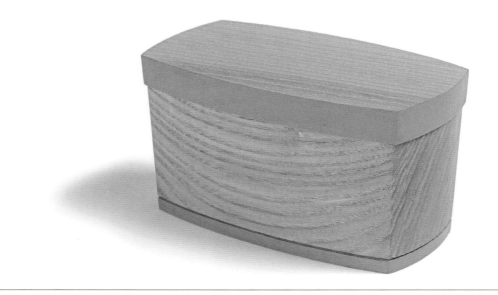

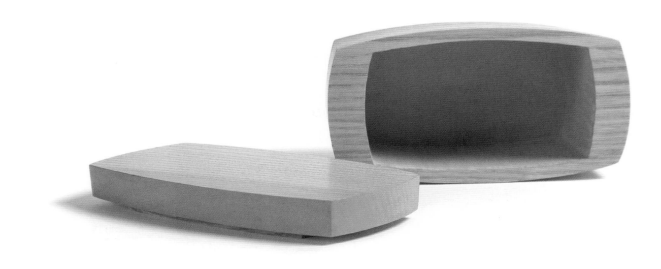

"Technical wizardry is always admirable, but aesthetic brilliance trumps it every time."

BOX 42

t took longer than I expected, but I finally made a bandsawn box using the techniques set out by Michael Cullen in his 2015 *Fine Woodworking* (issue #250) article. What's cool about his take on the bandsawn box is that he tilts the bandsaw table so that when he cuts the interior of the box it's narrower at the bottom than at the top. The waste created is tapered and can later be used to make a plug that becomes a seamless bottom for the box. This solves one of the biggest problems with bandsawn boxes: The blade removes material, and when you glue everything back together the parts really don't fit together quite right. You get gaps, misalignments, and the like. Cullen's technique overcomes the kerf. It's awesome. Of course, there is something far more awesome about his boxes: They are stunningly beautiful—light-years beyond every other bandsawn box that I've ever seen. Technical wizardry is always admirable, but aesthetic brilliance trumps it every time.

| SPECS |
- Ash
- Marigold yellow milk paint
- $2\frac{3}{8} \times 2\frac{3}{8} \times 4\frac{5}{16}$

So, I tilted the table about 3 degrees for this box and cut out the inside first, leaving the outside square (just as Michael does) for the glue-up. However, my plug didn't fit back into the box very well, due, I am sure, to my inadequacies as a craftsman. There were gaps, and I didn't want that. But like a lightning bolt, Box 41 came to mind. For that box, I used a piece of plywood (with shopsawn veneer on its bottom face) for the bottom. I rabbeted its top edge and then glued it to the bottom edges of the sides. It struck me that I could do that here, too. Using this style of bottom solved the kerf problem as well. More important—at least for me—the box looks like something I designed.

That's what I like about this box. It's significantly closer to being a box that fits into my aesthetic domain than the first two bandsawn boxes that I made (Boxes 9 and 16). Michael's technique partly explains that. The flared body (a consequence of tilting the table) adds elegance to the slightly arced sides. But it's also due to my willingness to chuck the notion that a bandsawn box has to be made by gluing all the parts back together. In this case, I've thrown out the bottom and created a more refined box in the process (by this I mean it's more refined than the box I would have made had I used the plug for the bottom). I don't have to play by the bandsawn box rules when I'm making one. You don't either. The result is greater conceptual and aesthetic freedom. I'm now much further down the road to making bandsawn boxes that are truly mine.

IT'S BEEN A LONG TIME
SINCE I USED A COLOR OF
MILK PAINT OTHER THAN
THE CUSTOM GREEN I MIX
UP. IT'S NICE TO SEE MY OLD
FRIEND, MARIGOLD YELLOW.
IT GOES NICELY WITH ASH,
BUT ONLY IF YOU PUT A BIT
OF SHELLAC ON THE ASH TO
AGE ITS COLOR.

BOX 42 | 161

BOX 43

This week brings another sugar bowl (Box 41 was the first). It's turned, giving it a more elegant look, and takes its inspiration from a variety of Japanese pottery I've seen. In particular, the shape of the bottom was informed by some small tea cups that I own. It's a beautiful shape. Fortunately, the bold lines running through the wood do not struggle against it. The wood is marblewood, which I've not used before. It's a tropical wood from South America (the northeast region, I believe), and this is heartwood. It's quite striking. It works fairly well, about the same as cocobolo. Because this box is meant to hold sugar (or salt), I painted the interior with marigold yellow milk paint, a nontoxic finish. I also happen to like the contrast between the wood on the exterior and the paint on the interior.

It was the painted interior that led to the lid's design. It sits down in the bottom, so that about $1/16$ in. of the side is visible above it. I thought that the yellow would create a delightful separation between the bottom and lid. I like this idea, and I'm pretty sure I'll return to it before I've completed all 52 boxes. Picking the wood for the lid wasn't too hard. The brown lines

| SPECS |
- Marblewood
- Walnut
- Marigold yellow milk paint
- 2¼ x 3 (dia.)

running through the marblewood immediately suggested walnut. Those lines tie the chocolate brown lid to the lighter, almost almond brown of the bottom. This is a good example of using woods that complement rather than contrast with one another. To determine the lid's arc, I quickly sketched out the body on some paper and then tried out several different arcs for the top. A low, relaxed arc seemed to work best. One last note about the lid. The underside is hollowed out a bit. I thought this would be more delicate and elegant than leaving it flat.

I didn't decide on the pull until after I had turned the lid. I typically use a third wood for my pulls (cocobolo being a favorite, along with apple). When the lid (or drawer front) is a dark wood like walnut, I use a lighter wood for the pull. However, if I used a wood like apple and left it natural, I'd be introducing a fourth color into the box. Instead, I painted the pull to match the yellow interior. It's a preview of the surprise awaiting you when you take the lid off. As for the shape, it's reminiscent of every pull I've ever turned. I think it goes nicely with the curves of the box body and lid.

SHAPING THE LID

It took two tries to get the lid right. The first one looked great on the outside, but I had no idea how to do the underside. I attempted to hollow it with my parting tool as I parted the lid from the turning blank. Not a good idea. For the second lid, I made a jamb chuck. The top of the lid was put against the jamb chuck, and I was able to hollow the underside with a gouge and get rid of the tenon I had used to hold the lid in a scroll chuck when I was shaping the top. Let me say this: Jamb chucks rock.

"The deep brown lines in the marblewood tie the chocolate brown of the walnut lid to the almond brown of the box."

BOX 43 | 165

"I strive for a purely emotional response. I want to speak to that part of us that feels beauty."

BOX 44

Here's another bandsawn box. The design is the same as Box 42, but this one is larger and made from cherry. I like it better. Because the box is taller, the sides appear to angle out more. They don't (it's the same angle on both boxes), but they appear to, and that's cool. Also, cherry—especially this particular piece of cherry—looks much better with marigold yellow milk paint than ash does. The proportions of this box are more elegant, I think. But there is also something about this box that I can't quite put my finger on. It simply strikes me as more appealing. It has something to do with the colors. The cherry, which is finished in a very light cut of shellac that barely affected its color, is so warm. It's the deep, rich, earthy red of aged cherry, but there is a hint of honey to it. And not just the color of honey, but the chatoyance of honey, too. Paired with the yellow milk paint, it's irresistible.

SPECS	> Cherry
	> Marigold yellow milk paint
	> $3^5/_8$ x $2^7/_{16}$ x $6^7/_{16}$

ON COLOR

There are three things that guide my design, and one of them is color. This particular piece of cherry paired with my beloved marigold yellow milk paint is almost too much. It's so important to pick good lumber when you're making a piece of furniture. You have to consider the species, the color, the cut (flat, rift, quarter), the tightness of the grain, the flow of the grain (in a gentle arc? dead straight? long cathedrals?), etc. You can absolutely make or break a piece when choosing lumber for it. This piece of cherry makes it. The color is tremendous. (The grain ain't so bad, either.)

Now I'm getting closer to what pleases me about this box. You see, I'm not talking about how it was made, but only about how it makes me feel. It's beautiful. It truly is. Everything else fades away. And that's what I strive for when making any piece of furniture or any box. I want to look at it, to feel its beauty and not think a lick about all the hard work, all the technique, the skill, and the knowledge that went into it. I strive for a purely emotional response. I want to speak to that part of us that feels beauty. When that happens I believe I've done something worthwhile, that I've made something that transcends the maker. It's a rare and perhaps fleeting accomplishment.

BOX 45

ox 45 is a tea box. The bottom drawer holds loose tea. The two top drawers hold tea packets. Behind the door is a cubby for a teapot and teacups. I don't drink tea, but I very much like the ritual of drinking tea. I don't have in mind the Japanese tea ritual (although this box clearly nods to Japanese design), but the ritual of afternoon tea at *Fine Woodworking*. It's a brief break in the day when most of the staff gets together to relax and talk. There is a clockwork to the way tea time happens: who boils the water, who sits (or stands) where, what we talk about, the jokes we make, etc. I love the work at the magazine, but I cherish the people I work with even more, and that's especially true at tea time. I made this box for them, from my fondness for them.

This box is nearly as big as the kindling box I made not too long ago, and takes its basic form from the kindling box, too. The case sits upon a base, separated by some spacers. Note that the middle spacer is in line with the divider between the door and drawers. Pleasant. Harmony. Had it been centered between the other two spacers it would have created a visual disconnect, and instead of blending quietly into the piece it would have been a jarring presence. The three spacers become part of the overall case structure, and the negative spaces they create contribute to the overall success of the box.

I SPECS I	› Cherry	› Snow white milk paint	› 15 x 8½ x 19
	› Basswood	› Fabric	
	› Cocobolo	› Thread	

The bottom drawer is shorter than the other two, but I think it works here. I was skeptical at first, because wider drawers at the bottom give a piece visual grounding. With this box, the base creates a sense of lightness and elevation, so it's OK that the bottom drawer is shorter. Like the base, it's helping to lift up the box. But if you take the two together, they are a solid foundation for the box. How does that work? It's the vertical divider between the door and two top drawers. The bottom drawer and base run the full length of the box. The space above them is divided, so you get a visual division between the bottom drawer/base and the upper part of the case. And here we come to the importance of varying the thickness of parts. The thickest parts are those on the perimeter of the case and base. The horizontal divider above the bottom drawer is slightly thinner. So too is the vertical divider separating the door from the two drawers on the right. They define the internal structure. The cocobolo divider between the two upper drawers is thinner still so that those two drawers are structurally subordinate. This variation in thickness creates a structural hierarchy that visually tells you that the base and bottom drawer are taken as a foundational pair even though they are separated by some beautiful negative space.

So, what about the door? It's made from basswood, which I chose because of its color and lack of any visible grain. I wanted the door to be about the fabric panel and lattice that overlays it. My friend and colleague Mike Pekovich has been experimenting with kumiko recently. As always, I feed off what he's doing. But traditional kumiko patterns would obscure the color of the fabric panel, so I went for a simple pattern based on rectangular negative spaces. This is much more in keeping with my design aesthetic. It's also in keeping with my propensity to take traditional material and design details and use them in very modern ways (milk paint, for example). I like how it turned out, and I plan to use latticework more often. I chose cocobolo for the frame to create some separation between the door and the lattice. It was a risk, but I think it worked out nicely. I had already decided to use cocobolo for the front edge of the divider between the two top drawers, and using it for the frame gave some unity between the two halves of the upper part of the case.

BOX 45 | 171

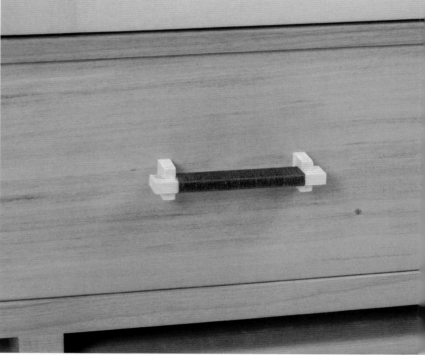

ON CHERRY

The grain runs up one side, over the top, and back down the other side. And almost all of the cherry in this box comes from a single 12/4 board. The drawer fronts are the exception. It's nothing but riftsawn cherry, too. That's the best kind of cherry. It allows the proportions and geometry of the piece to take precedence. It lets the bones stand forth. That's a good thing.

And cocobolo brings us to the pulls. All of their parts are ⅛ in. thick, like the parts of the latticework. The little feet have notches in them into which the bar fits. In this way they are tied to the kumiko. I then wrapped brown embroidery thread around the section between the feet (see the photos on pp. 180–181). The color of the thread ties the pulls to the cocobolo. (On a side note, these pulls are closely connected to the pull on Box 10 (see p. 59), because I got the idea for them from that box.) Also, the notion of a pull with cord or thread wrapped around it is something I've seen in Japanese furniture.

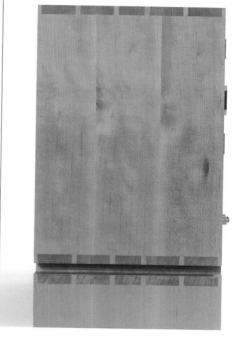

I PAINTED THE CUBBY
BEHIND THE DOOR WHITE
FOR TWO REASONS.
FIRST, A WHITE INTERIOR
IS BRIGHTER THAN ONE
THAT'S NATURAL CHERRY.
SECOND, A TEAPOT AND
TEACUPS STAND OUT IN A
MORE VISUALLY STRIKING
WAY AGAINST A WHITE
BACKGROUND.

BOX 45   173

MAKING KUMIKO FOR THE DOOR PANEL

1. Mark the length of the kumiko frame parts using the door as reference.

2. Cut the first notch in the inner frame parts.

3. Cut the second notch.

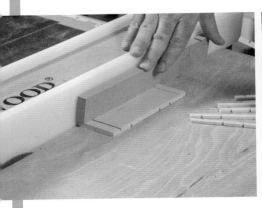

4. Rip the inner frame parts to width.

5. Glue together the outer frame.

6. Press the interlocking inner frame parts together.

7. Glue the inner frame to the outer frame.

8. Trim off the "horns."

9. Press the kumiko panel into the door.

BOX 46

This is the first of two boxes that I made using similar dimensions for the boxes themselves (that is, not including feet, lids, pulls, etc.). I even made both boxes from the same piece of cherry. Why? I wanted to see how different I could make them. (The second box is Box 47.)

Both boxes were designed to hold tea packets. I started from the known dimensions of a tea packet (it's a common size) and worked out from there. There are three slots for tea. These are created by a liner that is dry-fitted in the box. After adding up all of the involved dimensions (side thickness, liner thickness, top/bottom thickness, width and height of a tea packet, etc.), I knew the width, length, and height of the box. From there it was a matter of figuring out how to give each box its own unique soul.

SPECS	› Cherry	› Thread
	› Basswood	› 4½ x 4 x 9¼
	› Custom green milk paint	

The first two decisions I made about this box were that it would sit atop some type of foot structure and that I would not cut the sides apart to make a lid (as I did on Box 30, for example). I tackled the lid first. I went with an old friend: the lid that sits down in a rabbet cut into the inside face of the sides. A lid this big would need a substantial pull. Last week, I used some cool thread-wrapped pulls on a large tea cabinet. I decided to adapt that pull style to this box. This pull is much larger (the horizontal bar is 4½ in. long), which gave me enough meat to work with that I could bevel the ends of the pull and the ends of the feet. The bar and feet are made from basswood, and the thread is a brown embroidery thread (thicker is better for this purpose). I applied shellac to the basswood before wrapping the thread. I think the pull turned out quite well, and it's a style of pull that I'll continue to explore and develop.

BOX 46 | 177

ON BASSWOOD

The interior dividers are made from basswood. The more I use it, the more I like it. It's very soft, but the grain is nearly invisible, so it becomes just color and that makes it a wonderful tool. Grain too often fights against the shape, proportions, or color of a piece, at least when you're making small things.

For the sake of stability, I made the lid from plywood, gluing shopsawn veneers to the top and bottom faces. The veneers were cut from the same board as the sides. The plywood top also allowed me to glue the pull to the lid without any concern that wood movement might eventually pop the pull off. The edges of the lid are painted with a custom green milk paint, which creates separation between the lid and the sides. Without this bit of color, the lid and sides would simply melt into one another, because they're made from the same piece of wood. The color and grain match is perfect, and without the green you'd just have a big, indistinct blah. This little strip of color creates a border between the two, which allows the beautiful warmth of the cherry's color and its calm but elegant grain to really pop. The box is subtle and unassuming but still possesses a striking beauty. This approach appeals to me far more than slapping a wildly figured or super-contrasty wood on the box as a lid. (As I see it, the dependence on figured and contrasting wood is lazy design.)

After I figured out the lid and pull, it was easy to work out what the box would be sitting on. The feet are just a modified version of the pull. There are two long horizontal pieces and the feet are much longer, too. This design creates a balance between what's above and below the box. The bottom is plywood, which is important because the best (and most stable) way to attach the feet is to glue them on. If they had been glued to a solid-wood bottom, the bottom's movement definitely would have either pulled the feet apart or caused the bottom to split. So, plywood it is. There's a shopsawn veneer on the bottom face of the plywood. And like the feet themselves, the veneer is cut from the same piece of cherry as the box and lid. By the way, the top surface of the bottom is covered in a very nice fabric. Sure, you'll never see it because of tea packets. But it's there for the occasional glimpse, to show that every detail has been carefully considered.

WRAPPING THE PULLS

The way I secure the thread to the pull and how I wrap it around can be traced back to fly tying. I don't use any true knots. It's all a matter of securing both ends of the thread under the wrap. I can say that wrapping the pull was murder on my fingers. You must keep tension on the thread as it goes round. All of this tension is achieved through your fingers. It's tough work in that regard.

BOX 46 | 179

MAKING THE PULLS AND FEET

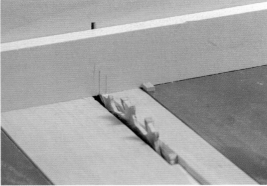

1 & 2. Clamp the notching jig (with attached tab) to the sled fence.

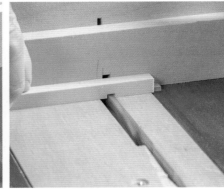

3. With the pull/feet blank registered against the tab, cut the first notch.

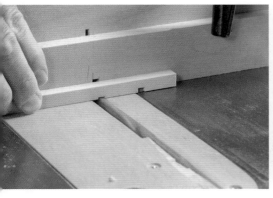

4. Place the first notch over the tab and cut the second notch.

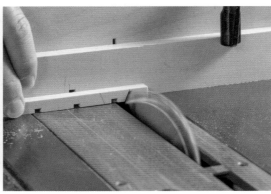

5. With the sawblade angled, cut the first beveled side of the foot. The notch is over the tab.

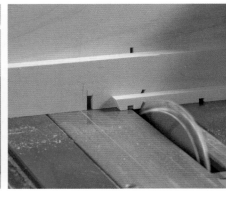

6. Cut the second beveled side of the foot. Again, the notch is over the tab.

7. Plane the bar of the pull to fit the notches in the two feet.

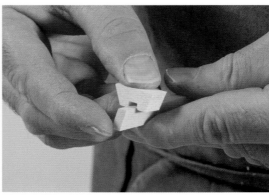

8. Fit the bar into the feet.

9. To prepare to wrap the pull, clamp the thread in a vise.

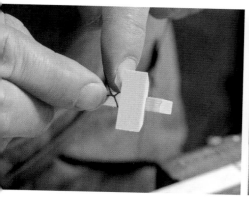

10. Start the wrap next to the inside edge of the foot.

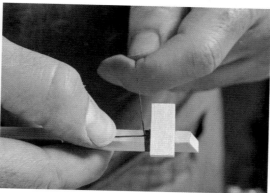

11. Continue wrapping the pull.

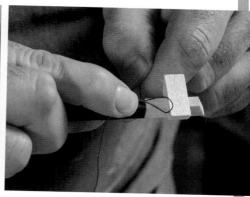

12. Form a loop in the thread and put it under the wrap.

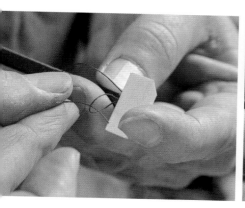

13. Thread the loose end of the thread through the loop.

14. Pull the loop back under the wrap.

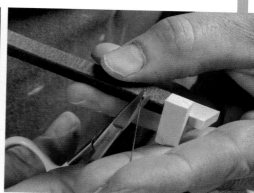

15. Cut off the excess thread.

BOX 46 | 181

"The box seems to float above the bottom."

BOX 47

Here's the second of the two boxes that I made using similar dimensions for the box body and the same species of wood (actually, both this box and Box 46 were made from the same board). I wanted to see how different, how unique, I could make two boxes that were the same box at their core. There was an easy way to make them different. I could have given one of them eight legs and a head, making it a spider box, or some other whimsical nonsense. I wanted more of a challenge, so I limited myself to variations in the lid, pull, and base. What's funny is that although I did make two boxes with unique souls, I also ended up with two boxes that are clearly from the hand of the same maker. I suppose that's really not surprising, but when I first put them next to one another I was struck by it. Actually, it makes me happy. I took a narrow set of design parameters and created two distinct boxes that are clearly expressions of my aesthetic. I didn't have to resort to outlandish and absurd differences to get the job done. A few subtle changes is all it took. I believe this means that I've grown as a designer and developed a better understanding of how to apply my aesthetic. This also means that my aesthetic is flexible, and this makes me happy, too (a point further illustrated by Box 45).

| SPECS |
> Cherry
> Cocobolo
> Custom green milk paint
> 4⅛ x 4 x 9¼

Well, that's enough philosophic ruminating. Let's get to the box at hand. I think that as I talk about what I was thinking as I designed this box I won't be able to avoid talking about the first box, but that should be instructive. I'll start with the pulls. On this box the "pull" is cocobolo banding that wraps around all four sides of the box. I made it just as I did the pull/lid keeper on Box 36. It's less than 1/16 in. proud of the sides, but this is more than enough for your fingers to get hold of and pull the lid off. This is a very different style of pull than the one I used on Box 46. But notice that this pull is cocobolo, and that I wrapped the pull for the first box in brown thread. Brown is a nice complementary color for the cherry box and green milk paint. It makes a great third color to introduce. Using it in the pull means that there will be less of it than both the warm, earthy reddish brown of the cherry and the lovely green milk paint. I'll admit that I chose cocobolo without thinking of the connection to the brown thread, but I certainly chose it for the same reasons that I went with brown thread. It's a strong wood that works well as a tertiary color. (As a primary or secondary wood, cocobolo becomes overbearing.) At any rate, the pull turned out to be something that both distinguished the second box from the first, but also connected the two.

On to the base. I've used this style before (Boxes 41, 42, and 44), and I'm starting to really like it. It's plywood with a shopsawn veneer on the bottom face and fabric on the top face. The edges are painted with the same custom green milk paint as the edges of the top. The bottom's edge is thicker than what you see of the top's edge, so the bottom has more weight and can anchor the box. I made this bottom a bit different than I did when I used it previously. The plywood portion of the bottom fits into a rabbet in the box. This means that there is a fairly deep rabbet around the top edge of the bottom, which results in a dark, distinct shadow line. The box seems to float above the bottom. I like it.

As for the top, I made it by gluing a panel into a rabbet and then cutting the box body in two. It's quite similar to, but still quite different from, the top I used for Box 46 (a panel that fits into a rabbet). The liner does not keep the lid in place, the pull does. As I did with the first box, I painted the edge of the panel to create separation between the box sides and the lid panel, and I did it for the same reason. It allows the panel to pop as if it were a second species or a highly figured piece of cherry, even though it's cut from the exact same board as the sides. The green creates a visual border around the panel.

GOOD DESIGN IS DELIBERATE

Look at that lovely little knot on the front of the box. This is how you use an imperfection. Don't put it smack dab in the middle, and don't try to emphasize more than one or a small cluster of them. Have the imperfection located off to one side, either up or down from center. This is a design choice that gets made when you're milling lumber. You've got to think that far out. As I've said before, there are no happy accidents. Good design is deliberate.

BOX 47 | 185

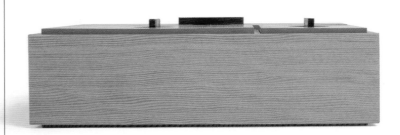

"Be deliberate with every choice, from initial design to finish."

BOX 48

made two of this box. One was for the 52 boxes project and the other was for the daughter of a friend who has given me a lot of great lumber over the last few years. When he gave me some wonderful vertical-grain Douglas fir recently, I decided to use it to make a box for his adorable little girl. The boards were left over from a sideboard he'd made for her room. He and I have very different styles, but the fact that the box and sideboard were made from the same boards holds the two together.

I know that doesn't say much about the design, but it's a part of this box's story. In fact, the wood is the origin of the box. I normally design and then pick lumber, but this time I was starting with the lumber and needed to develop a design that played to its strengths. I also needed more vertical-grain Douglas fir, because what my friend had given me was really only enough for one box. Fortunately, I once found a 3-in.-thick, 6-in.-wide, and 12-ft.-long piece of Douglas fir in the corner of a lumberyard. I bought it without a second thought. I'm glad I did, because it's got some figure to it, a lovely, warm color, and super-tight grain that's a bit wavy.

| SPECS |
> Douglas fir
> Cocobolo
> Custom green milk paint
> Fabric
> $1\frac{7}{8}$ x 6 x 6

At any rate, I was designing with vertical-grain Douglas fir in mind. What I wanted was a box that emphasized the tight, straight grain. This is no trouble on the sides. Make them rectangular, with the grain running the length. The lid is a different story. I knew that I wanted the box to have at least three compartments, because the three corresponding lids would allow me to play with the fir's grain. However, a box with overall rectangular dimensions limits the shape, size, and arrangement of the compartments. So, I went square. I think this is the first square box I've ever made. It's 6 in. square, to be exact. The narrow, full-width compartment is 2 in. wide, or one third of the box's overall width. The smaller of the two 4-in.-long compartments is 2 in. wide. The larger one is 4 in. square. These divisions make for compartments (and lids) that are well proportioned in themselves, in relation to one another, and in relation to the box's overall dimensions.

At the risk of putting even myself to sleep, here's a more detailed explanation of what's going on. The basic dimension of this box is 2 in. The sides are about 2 in. tall when you take the bottom and lid into account. The box is 6 in. square. That's three times the basic dimension, so there are three compartments. The dimensions for the compartments are all multiples of 2 in.

Back to the grain. The division and orientation of compartments allowed me to use the grain more boldly. It runs in one direction on the left side, and 90 degrees to that on the right side. Yet, because the grain is subtle, there's no uncomfortable tension created by this redirection. Somehow it's a dissonance that creates a harmony.

Well, that's a lot of talk about grain, proportions, and patterns. Let's talk about something else: the pulls. This is the second time I've used this pull on a box. What I like about it is the play between the circular mortise and the thin, rectangular pull. Combined, they create a nice visual set against the background of the tight, straight grain of the Douglas fir. The depth of the mortise allows me to use a pull that's very low but still gives enough grip (the pull extends down into the mortise). I don't mortise for the pull. Rather, it's T-shape, and the horizontal bar fits over the lid.

FOUR COLORS

Counting the primary color of the fabric, I've progressed to include four colors in my boxes. This is a good step forward. I think it works because the fourth color is hidden inside the box. Four colors on the outside would probably be too much. Which reminds me: If you ever get the urge to make a box using every scrap of figured and exotic wood in your shop, don't. It will be ugly, and your spouse will say she or he likes it only because she or he loves you and wants to spare your feelings. I choose my lumber carefully, and I'll quickly cut up a larger board to get to the grain I want. Be deliberate with every choice, from initial design to finish.

BOX 48 | 189

BOX 49

I made this box and the previous box to experiment with a few ideas before bringing them together in a third box, which will be one of the last two I make for the 52 box project. With Box 48, I was working on how to join two thin dividers. Here, I'm testing a theory on how to stack boxes. Perhaps you can decipher where I'm heading, but I won't say any more now. Let's get to the box at hand.

This box is actually three boxes that stack one on top of the other. The idea for it came from a conversation I had with Mike Pekovich. He was telling me about a type of box carried by samurai, called an *inro,* that was effectively a purse meant to carry coins and other small items. An *inro* is one of several boxes stacked atop the other and held together by cord. The cord is attached to the samurai's sash.

SPECS	> Cherry
	> Cocobolo
	> Fabric
	> 4¾ x 3 x 6

It sounded very cool, and on the spot I decided to make a set of stacking boxes. I just had no idea how to do it. A short time later I realized that many of the boxes I had been making in the 52 box project lent themselves to stacking, because I was using a rabbet in the top and bottom of the sides to hold the lid and bottom. If I made two boxes with the same dimensions and cut identically sized rabbets on the top and bottom on both boxes, the lid for one box would fit into the rabbet on the bottom of the other box. And the lid for the lower box would capture the box on top of it, holding the box in place. This is how these three boxes stack.

Of course, me being me, there had to be a shadow line between the boxes. So, the top two boxes have very thin bottoms, but not so thin that the box sits on the box sides beneath it. The lid of the lower box holds the upper box about $\frac{1}{16}$ in. above. And there's your shadow line. I like the shadow line here because it reveals that there are three boxes stacked rather than a single absurdly tall and narrow box. But that visual break between the boxes does something else, too. There is no grain

STACKING THE BOXES

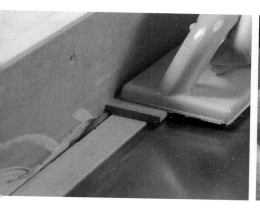

1. Cut the rabbets in the sides at the tablesaw.

2. Press the bottom into the box.

3. Plane the box tops to dial in the reveal between layers.

match as you move up from one box to the next. I didn't cut the sides from a wide board, in other words. This lack of match would have been noticeable had there been no space between the boxes, but it's really not with the shadow line there. That's a good thing.

When planning this box I knew that I wanted each box to have a different number of compartments, but before I gave any extended thought to this, I kicked around different proportions for the boxes themselves. I finally settled on a rectangle that's twice as long as it is wide. To keep the stacked boxes a reasonable height, I made the sides 1½ in. tall. After deciding on a fairly narrow rectangle, I knew that a divider along the boxes' length wouldn't be practical, because it would create two long and very narrow compartments. So, all of the dividers run across the width. After that it was a fairly quick trip to one box with one compartment, one with two compartments, and one with three. The compartments for the top box are not all the same size. The one in the middle is narrower. Why? Because cutting dadoes for the dividers in exactly the right location to end up with three equally sized compartments would be crazy hard. But cutting dadoes to make the two outside compartments the same size with a smaller (or larger) middle compartment is a snap. So, that's what I did. (I know this leaves a big question—Why is that true and how the heck did you do it?—hanging unanswered, but I beg your pardon, I never promised you a rose garden.)

BOX 49 | 193

IN THE PAST, WHEN I'VE MADE BOXES WITH COMPARTMENTS, I USED A BIRD'S-MOUTH JOINT TO JOIN THE DIVIDER TO THE BOX SIDES. I DID NOT DO THAT HERE. INSTEAD, I CUT A DADO IN THE SIDES THAT IS AS DEEP AS THE RABBET. THIS IS VERY EASY TO DO AND IT'S NO TROUBLE TO FIT A DIVIDER TO THE DADO AND THEN CUT ITS RABBETS. THIS TECHNIQUE IS WAY EASIER THAN FITTING A DIVIDER TO THE BIRD'S-MOUTH JOINT.

There was also the decision about which box would go on the bottom, which in the middle, and which on top. There is an argument for going three, two, one from the bottom up. However, a box with one compartment is a solid foundation because it's unbroken. So, it went on the bottom. The box with three compartments looks like three little boxes next to one another, so it went on top. And that's all I have to say about that.

Boxes 50 and 51 are already underway. I am going to finish. I am going to finish. So says the little steam engine that most probably could, I think.

BOX 49 | 195

"*The inward-sloping sides and painted edges are subtle things, but they make a big difference.*"

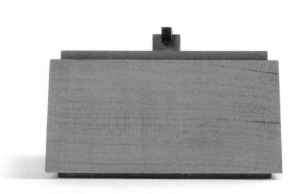

BOX 50

This one feels like a big deal. It's Box 50, after all, but I also think it's important because it's a refinement of a box that I've been making for several years: my old friend, the two-compartment box. It has smaller overall dimensions (1½ in. by 3 in. by 6 in. versus 2 in. by 5 in. by 8 in.), has one compartment instead of two, uses a more stylish pull, and has thinner sides and top. These differences make the box simpler and more delicate, but what makes it more elegant is the inward sloping sides and milk-painted edges on the top. These are subtle things, certainly, but they make a big difference. However, I'm kicking myself a bit, because had I used a slightly different pull, a slimmed-down version of the one I used on Box 46, this would be a perfect little box. I guess I'll have to make it again in the near future, just not before I finish the 52 box project. That's quickly coming to a close. And I already have the last two boxes designed (in fact, box 51 is just about done).

SPECS	› Cherry
	› Cocobolo
	› Custom green milk paint
	› Fabric
	› 1½ x 3 x 6

The inspiration for this box came from the second box I ever made (many, many years ago). It's at least 1 in. taller, and is closer to square in width and length. It also has sloping sides, but I made them by starting out with thick sides and planing the slope into them after assembly. This box has 3/16-in.-thick sides. There are compound miters at the corners that result in the inward slope. As I did for boxes 13, 14, and 15, I used a wedge to cut the compound miters, the rabbets, and the top and bottom edges. I like the technique because the wedge guarantees that all of the angles will be correct. As a result of the more refined construction, this box is more elegant than the original.

I'd like to say that a lot of careful thought went into the design of this box, but that wouldn't be true. I looked at the older box, asked how I would make it now, and the answer came to me quickly. Make it shorter, make it a rectangle, and use compound miters at the corners. I also used the bottom to create a shadow line. And the pull is similar to others that I've used. What I did, in other words, was take design details that I've been using this past year and put them together in a new way. In a way, there's nothing new here, but in truth it's a very new box. And it's one of my favorites. I love its delicacy, its elegance, and the beautiful fabric inside.

I should confess that the pull was originally made for Box 48. The design didn't work for that box, but it certainly does here. I like that the little feet are the same green that I used around the edge of the lid (and around the edge of the bottom, too, but you can't see it in any of the photos).

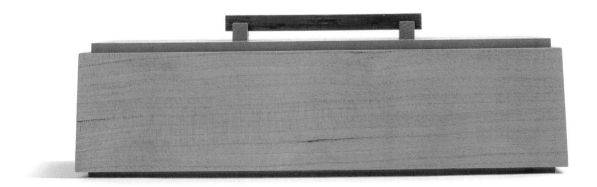

BOX 50 | 199

"There's a harmony between the three levels even though the base is visually striking."

BOX 51

I almost wish this was Box 52, because it brings together so much of what I've been doing for the past year that it's the perfect culmination for the 52 boxes project. It's certainly the best box I've made so far. (Actually, Box 52 is already done, so I think it's the best of all the boxes, too!)

The base is a good place to begin. The idea for a base like this one came to me one day while Mike Pekovich and I were driving back from lunch (sushi, I think). If I remember correctly, we were talking about kumiko and all the things you could do with it. Out of nowhere an image came into my mind, and I said, "I could make a box with a tall base and have kumiko wrap around it." I'm not sure what I had in mind then, but I was confident that it would look cool.

| SPECS | › Cherry
› Basswood
› Thread
› 8⅞ x 9 x 17

OK, so what was I thinking when I got around to developing the idea into an actual box? Well, the first thing I tackled was how tall the base needed to be in order to get a nice-looking kumiko pattern into it, and how that would affect the size of the case on top of it. I sketched out rectangles stacked on top of one another and experimented with different heights for them. A base that was slightly shorter than the "box" on top of it but as tall as or taller than the uppermost "box" looked right to my eye. What you end up with is a base that is tall enough for some nice kumiko to fit into it, but not so tall as to dominate the piece as a whole. There's a harmony between the three levels even though the base is visually striking. That's what I'm always after: something that has a lot of graphic punch but that isn't unbalanced.

So, after I figured out that business, I sketched out ideas for the two rows of drawers. I wanted a space on the right-hand side for a tea pot or some such thing, so I made the top row just a single drawer. The bottom row, I knew from previous experience with thin parts, couldn't be a single drawer. Thin parts like these tend to sag when they're longer than about 10 in., so I split the bottom row into two drawers. The wider one is 10 in. and the smaller one is about 7 in. wide. This told me that the top drawer should end in line with the wider bottom drawer.

BOX 51 | 203

ON DESIGN

This box has brought home a hunch that's been developing in me for quite some time. It's tremendously difficult to dissect what goes into good design and present it in a linear fashion. Like nature, design is a web of connected points. You can pick one as a starting point, but it's really just one point in an inextricably bound set of nonlinear decisions, all of which are needed to explain any particular one.

The width of the drawers is a result of determining how much space I would need on the right side to put a small tea pot or some other little piece of pottery. Based on some pieces that I own, I figured 7 in. would suffice. Some sketches told me that 10 in. on the other side would look nice. From there, it was a matter of determining how tall the bottom drawers needed to be so that they could hold loose tea (left side) and tea packets (right side). The top drawer is for pennies, acorns, and tales of adventure.

OK, so what about the kumiko pattern? I wanted something geometric but not so crowded that it would obscure the fabric behind it. That meant a lot of negative space. I wanted two horizontal kumiko pieces between the frame and spaced them asymmetrically (more space between them than at the top and bottom) to let the fabric show through more prominently. The vertical pieces are done in pairs, because I knew that it would look better than to do them individually. (Of course, there was some sketching involved, too.) The vertical pattern for the front/back had to be different from the pattern for the sides because the front and back aren't a multiple (in length) of the sides. So, I started them the same on the ends (a pair of vertical pieces 1 in. from the ends and spaced ⅝ in. apart), but the sides just have two single pieces between the pairs at the ends. I divided the space between the two pairs into thirds because there are three pairs of verticals between the two end pairs on the front and back. How did I figure all of this out? Magic 8 Ball and rum. Or was it rum, then Magic 8 Ball?

All of the cherry for this box came from a single 12/4 board. I resawed it to create ⅜-in.-thick boards from the edge grain. I then glued up three of these new boards to create the panels for the sides. These boards ended up being mostly quartersawn and heavily figured. Actually, the entire 12/4 board was heavily figured, even on the flatsawn faces. I hate figure. It's a pain to machine and plane, and can be distracting. And I think folks lean on figure as a crutch to make otherwise bad design somewhat attractive. It works OK here, though, because the design is good.

"Like nature, design is a web of connected points."

BOX 51 | 205

MAKING THE BASE

1. Cut a groove into the frame parts.

2. Miter the frame parts.

3. Glue up the frames.

4 & 5. Notch the frames to accommodate the "legs."

6. Set strips of wood into the grooves.

7. Glue the frames to the inner plinth.

8 & 9. Glue and clamp in the legs.

10. Pare the leg length flush to the frame.

11. Plane the leg thickness flush to the frames.

BOX 51 | 207

"There is always something new that can be incorporated into a seasoned aesthetic."

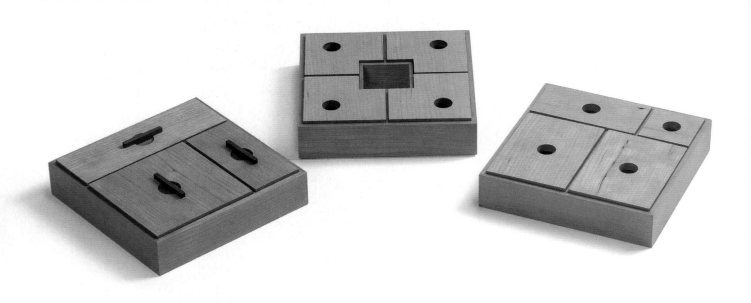

BOX 52

ox 52. Done. And that's all I have to say about that.

Kidding. I always have plenty to say. This is another stacking box, like Box 49, but I changed the shape from rectangle to square, taking Box 48 as my starting point (I really like Box 48). I think Box 49 is too tall, so this time I made the sides 1¼ in. tall instead of 1½ in. I know it's impossible to tell from these photos, but the lower height is an improvement. I also like the square format for the boxes. (I'm actually excited about designing more square boxes in the future. I can't believe I never tried a square box until Box 48.) The biggest benefit of the square is that I had more latitude in dividing the boxes into compartments. For the top box, I used the same arrangement as I did for Box 49. For the middle box, I added a compartment. For the bottom box, I added another compartment, but not another lid. A square compartment in the middle of a box with others wrapping around it: I've had this arrangement in mind for years. It wasn't as hard to do as I feared. I did not use a lid for it because I wanted a pop of color in the middle and I thought fabric would be cooler than a painted lid.

| SPECS | > Cherry
> Custom green milk paint
> Fabric
> 4⅜ x 6½ x 6½

I like that this little compartment without a lid is in Box 52. The box incorporates a great deal of what I learned as I made the other 51 boxes, but also has something new—the compartment without a lid. It's a bit of a harbinger, I think. Sure, I've made a lot of boxes, but I haven't exhausted my design resources. There is always something new that can be incorporated into a seasoned aesthetic. Chosen carefully, a new detail can bring fresh life to a body of work that's mature and well defined.

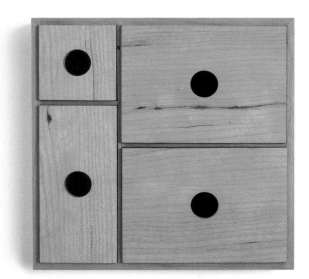

THE INSIDE EDGES OF THE FINGER HOLES ARE PAINTED WITH GREEN MILK PAINT, AS ARE THE UNDERSIDES OF THE BOTTOMS ON THE TOP TWO BOXES.

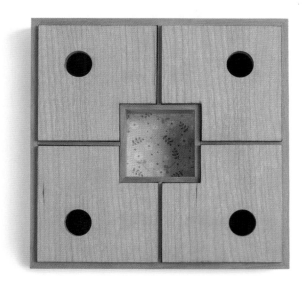

BOX 52 | 211

AFTERWORD

Almost two years have passed since I completed Box 52. As I look back on my year of making 52 boxes, the first thought that comes to mind is this: I made a lot of boxes. I have nowhere to keep them all. Fortunately, I have a nice solution.

I have begun to give them away, and this makes me happy, because the folks I have been giving the boxes to genuinely appreciate them. This feels good, and helps me to understand the project and myself in a more meaningful way. Sure, I was looking to improve my design skills. But why was I doing that? I now know that it's because what I really want from woodworking is to make something beautiful, but not something that only I see as beautiful.

Part of what it means to be human is to have an emotional response to beauty, and I want to stir that emotion in other people, especially the ones that I know and care for. Life is better in those moments when our hearts beat a bit faster, a bit more joyously, because something truly beautiful has crossed our eyes. I don't know if any of my boxes are that beautiful (I doubt it), but I'll keep making boxes and furniture in the hope that I eventually make one thing that is that beautiful. If I can bring even a small bit of joy and happiness into the life of another person, I'll consider my time in the shop well spent.

METRIC EQUIVALENTS

INCHES	CENTIMETERS	MILLIMETERS	INCHES	CENTIMETERS	MILLIMETERS
⅛	0.3	3	13	33.0	330
¼	0.6	6	14	35.6	356
⅜	1.0	10	15	38.1	381
½	1.3	13	16	40.6	406
⅝	1.6	16	17	43.2	432
¾	1.9	19	18	45.7	457
⅞	2.2	22	19	48.3	483
1	2.5	25	20	50.8	508
1¼	3.2	32	21	53.3	533
1½	3.8	38	22	55.9	559
1¾	4.4	44	23	58.4	584
2	5.1	51	24	61	610
2½	6.4	64	25	63.5	635
3	7.6	76	26	66.0	660
3½	8.9	89	27	68.6	686
4	10.2	102	28	71.7	717
4½	11.4	114	29	73.7	737
5	12.7	127	30	76.2	762
6	15.2	152	31	78.7	787
7	17.8	178	32	81.3	813
8	20.3	203	33	83.8	838
9	22.9	229	34	86.4	864
10	25.4	254	35	88.9	889
11	27.9	279	36	91.4	914
12	30.5	305			

If you like this book, you'll love *Fine Woodworking*.